P9-DMV-947

WINNING THE RAT RACE

WINNING THE RAT RACE

DR. KEVIN LEMAN

A JANET THOMA BOOK

THOMAS NELSON PUBLISHERS
Nashville • Atlanta • London • Vancouver

Copyright © 1996 by Dr. Kevin Leman

All rights reserved. Written permission must be secured from the publisher to use or repro-
duce any part of this book, except for brief quotations in critical reviews or articles.

Published in Nashville, Tennessee, by Thomas Nelson, Inc., Publishers, and distributed in
Canada by Word Communications, Ltd., Richmond, British Columbia.

Unless otherwise noted, Scripture quotations are from THE NEW KING JAMES
VERSION. Copyright © 1979, 1980, 1982 Thomas Nelson, Inc., Publishers.

Scripture quotations noted NIV are from the HOLY BIBLE, NEW INTERNATIONAL
VERSION®. Copyright © 1973, 1978, 1984 by International Bible Society. Used by permission of Zondervan Publishing House. All rights reserved.

Library of Congress Cataloging-in-Publication Data

Leman, Kevin.
    Winning the rat race without becoming a rat : the psychology of winning in business /
Kevin Leman.
        p.   cm.
    Includes bibliographical references.
    ISBN 0-8407-3491-3
    1. Success in business—Psychological aspects. 2. Personality and occupation. 3. Birth
order. I. Title.
HF5386.L656 1996
650.1—dc20   96-14886
                                                     CIP

Printed in the United States of America.

1 2 3 4 5 6 — 01 00 99 98 97 96

*T*his book is affectionately dedicated
to my big brother, Jack.
(Actually it's Dr. John E. Leman, Jr.)
I think Dad must have liked him best.

*Jack, you've paved so many ways for me
in life. You're still my idol.
You taught Moonhead Dietsch and me our
very first lessons about the opposite sex.
(No wonder we have five children,
including a four-year-old!)
You beat up the neighborhood bully for
me on more than one occasion and
cleaned out my bloody knee.
But beyond that, you've been a great brother.*

*God blessed you with lovely Linda and three
great kids, Andy, Wendy, and Daniel.
I love all of you.*

CONTENTS

PART I

Could Something Like Birth Order Actually Work in *My* Business?

In business it's not only IQ that matters; it's not necessarily great transactions that matter, but there are a lot of what I call "softer sides" that can make the difference between success and failure. Birth order is one of those. It has, for example, helped me win people over and make them allies on my team to help keep the ship afloat.

—MICHAEL LORELLI
PRESIDENT-AMERICAS, TAMBRANDS, INC.

If All the Psychologists in the World Were Laid End to End, Would You Leave Them There?

Okay, so I'm starting with maybe two strikes on me: First, I can almost hear you thinking it: *What is a family and marriage therapist doing writing a book about business?* So, right from the get-go, I want to make it clear this is not a book about how, when, and where to buy pork bellies; or the hottest new mutual fund.

Second, I realize some people have rather dim opinions about my profession. You may be among those who would agree with the clever person who once said, "If you took all the psychologists in the world and laid them end to end around the earth, it would be a pretty good idea to just leave them there."

I concur—at least in part. A lot of us psychologists are stuffy, boring, and impractical. It's also very true that there are few psychologists who don't need one themselves.

But despite all those hurdles, I still believe I have something that you need—something that could be summed up in a brief conversation I had with the president of a fair-sized manufacturing firm who has read many of the business best-sellers and attended motivational seminars and workshops, ad infinitum. When I asked him what his company was finding in the young employees they were hiring, his answer was brief:

"Not much."

I knew what he meant. As I do the public-speaking and the talk-show circuits, I often fly with a CEO or VP in charge of marketing in the next seat. We talk about a lot of things, but it usually boils down to how businesses and corporations are all looking for the same thing: how to motivate their people to do the best job possible, and even make some money at the same time!

*T*he more you know and understand about how humans tick—including yourself—the more equipped you will be to compete in that rat race called the "marketplace."

That's why I believe every business person alive needs to be a psychologist of sorts. If you are in business and don't understand this, it's high time you did. Psychology is, after all, simply the study of human thinking and behavior. The more you know and understand about how humans tick—including yourself—the more equipped you will be to compete in that rat race called "the marketplace." And the more you know about how people want to be treated, the more truly successful you will be.

What I Learned Selling Magazines to "Suckers"

Strangely enough, I discovered the value of basic psychology in business long before I ever became a psychologist. It was one of those "Aha!" kind of things—the light dawned and I saw something I needed to see much more clearly. Or perhaps I really saw it for the first time.

It was spring, and I had arrived in Tucson, home of the University of Arizona Wildcats. Somehow, I had been able to enroll in this fine institution despite the sorry record I had compiled at a small college in the Midwest where I had eked out a C average during my freshman year by making use of the well-known "fear factor" (fear of having to go to work). During my sophomore year, however, all the wheels had come off. First I had started flunking courses and then my roommate and I pulled off a prank that left the college dean totally unamused.

He called me in for a short but not too sweet conversation. I left his office with a very firm invitation to leave school and not come back. Because my parents had just moved to Tucson to escape the bitter winters of the Buffalo, New York, area, I quickly migrated in that direction.

Upon my arrival the only work I could find was a job as a janitor at the Tucson Medical Center, working forty hours a week for $195 a month. It didn't take me long to figure out this was really not what I wanted to do with my life. Because I knew I could hack college work if I "really tried," I enrolled at the U of A in a night course, which I promptly flunked. Undaunted, I tried again and, because I needed some money to finance my college work, I also got a job selling magazines door-to-door for a company whose name has long since faded from my memory.

To learn how to peddle magazines, I took an intensive training course that lasted all of one afternoon. The basic "pitch" included walking up to the door, and when someone answered we were to say: "Hi! You're probably very busy, but could I just take a minute of your time? We are conducting a research analysis for a nationally known firm, and because we're in your neighborhood today, we'd just like to have you tell us what four magazines on this list you would like to have absolutely free."

If we could get the person to take the card, which listed dozens of magazines, and start looking at it, we knew we had a chance. And when the customer picked the four magazines he or she wanted "absolutely free," we knew we practically had a sale.

One very important requirement, however, was that we get "the front"—seven dollars down payment on three more subscriptions the customer had to buy in order to get the other four free. We were taught to say, "That's right, it's $7.00 down and $2.95 a month." What we were taught *not* to mention, however, was that the customer would pay $2.95 a month for twenty-six months.

Simple multiplication tells you that totals out at an additional $76.70, meaning the customer was really paying a total of $83.70 for the seven magazine subscriptions: the three he was buying and the four "free" ones. There was nothing new about this kind of approach. We were getting people to buy on impulse. All we wanted them to hear was "$7.00 down and $2.95 a month."

We weren't exactly lying to our customers; we just weren't giving them all the information. And they still were getting a good deal—seven magazines at what amounted to almost twelve dollars a year for each magazine.

In 1962, $83.70 was not exactly small change, and the research analysis approach to peddling magazines was a tough sell, particularly when you found a customer who had sense enough to ask, "$2.95 a month for *how many* months?"

Undaunted by the odds against finding customers who could be fooled by the "get four free and buy three more" approach, I reported back the next morning and was driven out to a middle-class Tucson neighborhood for my first day of work. I was dumped on a corner and told, "Okay, be back here by 1:00 P.M. sharp."

I began knocking on doors, giving my pitch, and taking orders, complete with the seven dollars up front. The morning seemed to fly by, and when I looked at my watch I saw it was time to get back to my pickup corner. Back at the office I handed my orders to my immediate supervisor, a lady named Joyce. I thought I had done pretty well, and I was anxious to see what she would say. Joyce looked at the sheaf of papers in her hand and said, "What are *these*?"

"Well, they're my orders," I replied, wondering if somehow this wasn't enough.

"You mean, you got *all* these orders this morning?" she said incredulously.

"Yep," I said with a sheepish smile.

"Come with me," she directed, and we walked back to the manager's office. She waved the orders in front of the manager and said, "Larry, look! Look at what Calvin did!"

I was feeling so good I didn't even bother to correct her on my name. She was holding *twenty-seven orders* for magazines, a new one-morning record for Tucson, if not the entire nation as far as that company was concerned.

I Always Brought My "Dancin' Shoes"

What was the secret of my magazine selling success? As I look back, I see several things that were in my favor. A lot of my customers were housewives who may have felt sorry for this young man in the University of Arizona T-shirt who stood there sweating on the doorstep, trying to explain that he "really wasn't selling anything, just doing research and making a really wonderful opportunity available."

Of course, that line was old even way back then. With some people it worked and with many it didn't. But I had a knack for spotting the ones who would waver, and with a few more comments about what a "great deal" this was, I'd get them to invite me in. It helps to remember that this was the early '60s and crime wasn't anything like it is today. People were far more trusting and I don't think it hurt me to be wearing that Wildcat T-shirt. The Wildcats have always been "the only game in town" as far as Tucson is concerned and, if I came from the U of A, surely I was a "nice young man."

So I'd often wind up in the living room, hearing apologies for how messy things were, and assuring the lady of the house that she had a lovely home and I was happy to be there. Next, I'd usually be offered something to drink and, of course, I immediately asked if I could help with anything. I was always very service oriented, even before I realized what "service oriented" meant. I guess I had picked that up from the way I was reared by my mother, as well as my sister, Sally, eight years my senior.

As I'd sit there sipping lemonade or drinking coffee, I'd push for a decision, but I was never pushy. Clearly, I wasn't the threatening type. I never huffed and puffed, trying to blow the door down. I'd go in with a soft sell, but I also "brought my dancin' shoes" and, more often than not, I left with an order.

I'm sure my baby-of-the-family personality gave me an edge. As the last born in the family with a super-capable big sister and brother above me, I always knew I couldn't compete with either of them academically or athletically. So I became the family mascot. Actually, my parents helped me in that direction by nicknaming me "Cub" when I was only eleven days old. The nickname stuck, and, as I grew up, I made the most of my cublike status by becoming the family clown and comedian.

All my life I had been cute, funny, and easy with people in new situations. I could often make them laugh, even when there didn't seem to be anything to laugh about. While selling magazines I remember coming up to one door where a sign said, "Unless you're a friend, don't knock on this door." Naturally, I went ahead and knocked on the door. A bleary-eyed gentleman answered, looking as if I had just gotten him off his couch. He gave me a sour look and said, "Yeah?"

Swallowing hard, I decided to talk fast: "Oh, hi! I just read your sign, and I had no way of knowing if you were a friend until I took a look at you."

The man stared at me for several long seconds and then he laughed. We had a brief conversation and he didn't buy any magazines, but when he shut the door, he was chuckling.

My "Success" Taught Me a Valuable Lesson

But what, you may be wondering, was the valuable "discovery" I made while selling magazines as a college student? After my record first day, I went on for several more weeks, continuing to do well. And then something started to bother me. Yes, I was a success—I saw that I could continue selling magazines and make some pretty decent money for a college kid. But after being there almost two months, I had the gnawing feeling I had made a mistake. I had been overzealous in doing just what the company had asked me to do. I wasn't robbing people, but it was all just a little too slick. I was taking advantage of people's natural desire to "get a good deal."

When I told Joyce I was quitting, she looked at me incredulously and said, "Why? You're the best salesman we've got. You're doing very well and you're just a kid."

I told Joyce I appreciated knowing I was the best sales person she had and I really enjoyed selling. But getting people to spend eighty-four dollars on magazines they didn't necessarily need or want was starting to bother me.

Joyce just looked at me and shrugged. "Sorry to lose you, Kevin," she said. "You're really good—a natural-born salesman if I ever saw one."

As I left the dingy apartment that served as the magazine sales office, I had mixed emotions. In two months of selling door-to-door—one of the toughest gigs you could ever ask for—I had discovered I was a natural-born salesman, but I had also realized that I had a conscience. It was nice that Joyce had finally gotten my name right, but did she think I was going to waste my talent and would never amount to anything? But where could I find a job that would pay as well as selling magazines?

Deep down, however, I knew I had made the right decision. From that day forward, I decided that I'd use my talents not to slicker people but to serve them, and I have never been sorry. My magazine selling experience taught me a basic premise that I still use today. I could try to state it in "business speak," but I'd rather use Lemaneze:

LEMAN'S LAW #1:

There has to be more to making money than making money.

In other words, whatever you do, be sure it provides a service—something of real value to others. And whatever product or service you provide, offer it with the right motive—wanting the best for your customers, not trying to slip one past them. You need to take the time to know your customers as people, not just potential sales figures.

Now I realize this is not exactly an original idea. It's been around for years, and you can find it in all kinds of business books today. But like so many of the basics, this concept of putting people ahead of things, especially that thing called money, gets neglected. So, to start out, I want to go back to square one. No matter what you do in the business world, making money involves a lot more than just making money. You need to know who you are selling to, who you are working with, and who is working for you. And that's why I say every business person needs to be part psychologist, which, as I will show you, is easier than you might think.

Harvey Knows Psychology

One of my favorite business writers is Harvey Mackay, who has written several best-sellers, including *Swim With the Sharks*

Without Being Eaten Alive. Early in his first chapter, he writes: "Knowing your customer means knowing what your customer really wants. Maybe it is your product, but maybe there's something else, too: Recognition, respect, reliability, concern, service, a feeling of self-importance, friendship, help . . ."[1]

Mackay believes that these "other things" are what we really care about. Sometimes, says Mackay, these intangibles are even more important than the bottom line. I couldn't agree more and would only add that what Harvey is talking about are values—the things that are really meaningful to most of us.

When I caught up with Harvey Mackay, he was between planes, "on top of a tiger," as he put it, after spending six weeks pulling together a $125 million deal to keep the Minnesota Timberwolves in Minneapolis. The Wolves had been making noises about moving to New Orleans and Harvey, who had already done some herculean work to keep the Minnesota Twins in town back in the '80s, was again right in the middle of a public service campaign to keep a pro franchise in the Twin Cities.

Was he going to all this trouble simply because he liked basketball? Possible but doubtful. Was he giving all this time free of charge because Minneapolis/St. Paul just happens to be the home of the Mackay Envelope Corporation, as well as the community in which Harvey grew up? Partly true, perhaps, but there had to be more to it than that.

And then it hit me; I had contacted Harvey Mackay to pick his

*K*nowing your customer means knowing what your customer really wants. Maybe it is your product, but maybe there's something else, too: Recognition, respect, reliability, concern, service, a feeling of self-importance, friendship, help . . .
—Harvey Mackay, Chairman and CEO, Mackay Envelope Corporation; Author, Swim With the Sharks Without Being Eaten Alive

brain, but before I had been able to ask him my first question, he was modeling for me the very values he trumpets in his best-selling books. He was talking about those intangibles that have to do with helping others feel recognized and respected because of his concern and service.

Harvey Mackay could have reluctantly turned down requests to help keep the Timberwolves in Minneapolis—after all, he had enough things going to keep any CEO busy thirty-six hours a day. But instead, he had poured himself into the challenge on what he told me was "an eight-days-a-week basis" because he knew how valuable a pro franchise can be to a city. Not only is it good for business; it is good for the public psyche, so to speak. Anything that helps foster loyalty and pride in a community will eventually result in a better economy—and a better community.

But it's my guess there was even more than that to Harvey's "madness." He had worked hard to keep the Timberwolves in Minneapolis simply because he actually believes what he writes and tries to live it. He wants to serve, to help, because he knows that this is what makes everyone a winner.

The more I listened to Harvey talk, the more I realized he was a psychologist, par excellence, because he understands that you have to deal with people in a way that is *consistent with how they view life*. Twenty years of being a psychologist and counselor have convinced me that unless you approach people by recognizing *their* needs, *their* desires, and *their* values, you won't even get up to bat, much less to first base.

Why I Wrote This Book

After my brief but ambivalent career as a magazine salesman, I went on to get bachelor's, master's, and doctorate degrees—all from the University of Arizona. It was there that I learned how people tick and how the human personality is formed by certain powerful influences that play an important role in making you who you are today.

One of these powerful influences is *birth order*. A few pages back I mentioned my "baby personality" as being a real asset in selling. My order of birth—last in a family of three children—actually equipped me to be a good salesman. In Chapter Three, I'll explain why it's no coincidence that birth order studies show last borns often wind up in sales or other people-oriented jobs.

*B*irth order will help you understand yourself—*why you are the way you are*—as well as understand others—*why they are the way they are*—and how you can deal with them more effectively.

Now you may have heard of "birth order" and, then again, maybe you haven't. Put briefly, birth order is the science of understanding your particular limb on the family tree. Were you born first, second, third, or even farther down the line? Wherever you landed, it has affected your life in countless ways. Throughout my career as a psychologist I've used the theory of birth order almost daily to help people understand themselves and solve their problems.

And over the years I've used birth order concepts in other settings besides marriage and family. Much of my speaking has been done with corporations and businesses, including the IBM School of Management, the Williams Companies, Pepsi, and Pizza Hut. In addition, I have appeared before groups such as the "Million Dollar Round Table," the "Top of the Table," and the "Young Presidents' Organization," where salaries range up to the high six figures, and more.

My feedback has been so positive that I decided to write a book that would focus on building relationships by learning what your customer, employee, or boss really wants and needs. As you go about building business relationships, a basic understanding of birth order characteristics can come in handy—and then some.

I am so sure about the value and practical applications of birth order that I'm not afraid to step into the business arena to share with you tips and insights about human nature that will enable you to sell better, manage better, or work better in any setting where business is being conducted. Birth order will help you understand yourself—*why you are the way you are*—as well as understand others—*why they are the way they are*—and how you can deal with them more effectively.

In short, you will master some new techniques for running successfully in the great competition all of us face every morning—the rat race. We all seem to be in the rat race whether we like it or not. As Harvey Mackay puts it, "It isn't just dog eat dog out there; it's what Ray Kroc, the founder of McDonald's, called, 'rat eat rat.'"[2] The bad news is that, in all too many cases, Ray is right. The good news, however, is that you can use the tips in this book to succeed without having to stoop to becoming a rat yourself.

Does the Golden Rule Really Pay Off?

But please understand one thing: I want to help you have an edge, but not an unfair advantage. There will always be those who are willing to use the information in a book like this to shade the truth or stack the deck in order to come out on top. I'm betting, however, that you know from experience what I know: The more we understand about how we tick and how other people tick, the more we will want to treat others in the way we would like to be treated.

After counseling thousands of people, I know beyond a shadow of a doubt that the Golden Rule is not only the best and right way to go, it's the most practical. It pays off. Interestingly enough, there are many business people of the '90s who seem to feel the same way. Recently I obtained a transcript from ABC's *World News Tonight with Peter Jennings* that featured what Jennings called "the growing tendency of business leaders in America to have their personal faith make an impact in their companies. In other words, they are using the Bible as a guide to business."

One of the businessmen quoted on the program was John Beckett, successful Ohio manufacturer of oil burners. Beckett said, "I see my role in the world to take what I believe as a Christian and translate that into practical day-to-day expressions of what I believe."[3]

Because my own spiritual orientation is the same as Beckett's, I eagerly read on. I never push my faith on anyone, but I'm always trying to live it

I think [the Golden Rule] is a reaction to an ethic of greed that kind of took hold of business in the '80s. Now you see a sense of emptiness; that, "Gee, maybe there's a little more to life than just my bank account."
—*Lauren Nash,*
Professor of Business Ethics,
Boston University

on a practical basis, so I was interested in anything else Beckett might have to say. I was pleasantly surprised when I learned that his faith teaches him that family comes before work and he makes sure his employees don't put in too many hours at the office!

Then the transcript went on to quote Lauren Nash, a professor of business ethics at Boston University, who had somewhat skeptically researched business leaders who mixed faith and profit making. Could religion literally be part of someone's business life? Or was it all just hypocritical sham?

On *World News Tonight* Professor Nash stated that her research shows literally thousands of business leaders across the nation are struggling to integrate their very private world of faith into the competitive world of work. Her explanation: "I think it is a reaction to an ethic of greed that kind of took hold of business in the '80s. Now you see a sense of emptiness; that, 'Gee, maybe there's a little more to life than just my bank account.'"[4]

According to the *World News Tonight* transcript, it seems to be happening everywhere and across denominational lines. Orthodox Jews on Wall Street are breaking away from the office to study the Talmud; the Christian Businessmen's Committee has fifteen thousand members who usually meet at sunup to pray for help on everything from employee problems to marketing strategies. And there is also the Fellowship of Companies for Christ, an organization for hundreds of chief executive officers who struggle with the burdens of leadership.

I was chuckling as I laid the news transcript down. Even in the skeptical, cynical business world of the '90s, the Golden Rule is alive, well, and wielding a powerful influence.

"C'mon, Doc, Does Birth Order Really Make Sense?"

Obviously, I'm not trying to equate birth order with the Golden Rule, but I know from experience that a working knowledge of birth order can help make you much more skilled in treating others as you yourself would like to be treated. I also know that the birth order theory has its critics and skeptics. Everywhere I go I often hear "C'mon, Doc, this birth order stuff can't be for real. . . . it all sounds too simplistic." I just smile and ask them to hear me out and when they do, they usually change their tune.

My converts include top officers, sales managers, and sales reps from many of America's premier corporations. Mike Lorelli, former president of Pizza Hut International and Pepsicola East, became a believer when he read *The Birth Order Book* on a plane. That led to his invitation for me to speak to a group of his top executives. Today he still orders *The Birth Order Book* by the caseload and distributes it to his employees.

Currently Lorelli is president-Americas of Tambrands, Inc., which employs over two thousand people. When I asked him for a few of his thoughts about birth order and why it's a worthwhile tool in the business world, he told me: "I guess I begin by saying everybody who is important to me was born. And when you think about it that way, you can use birth order to categorize people and try to figure out what's the best way to motivate your customers, suppliers, consumers, bosses, peers—whoever."

Mike's words told me that he just didn't skim *The Birth Order Book* and smile at some of the amusing stories and observations. He really got the message. Then he went on to say:

"In business it's not only IQ that matters; it's not necessarily great transactions that matter, but there are a lot of 'softer sides' that can make the difference between success and failure. Birth order is one of those. It has, for example, helped me win people over and make them allies on my team to help keep the ship afloat."

I love what Mike says about birth order being one of the "softer sides" that spell the difference between success and failure. Selling this kind of "softer side" is why I love getting up in front of a bunch of jaded vice-presidents and sales managers who greet me with arms and legs crossed, body language clearly saying, "*What* have they got for us *now*?"

An hour or so later, however, the arms and legs are uncrossed and the lights are going on in blank faces as I help them see why understanding your own birth order and the birth order of the person you are dealing with can be so powerful. Not only does it enhance business relationships, but it helps you create win/win situations for everyone, no matter what kind of deal you are trying to make.

Business People Have Two Goals

Business people are really like everybody else. They have two goals in life: to be successful and to be happy. The rub is that it is hard to be both. Too often businessmen and -women have to sacrifice personal values and convictions in order to compete and win in the marketplace. But unless you live congruently with your personal values, you will never be happy. You'll always have that vague feeling that you've been a rat, are a rat, or are about to become a rat. The good news is, you don't have to be a rat to win in business. By understanding those you deal with, you can win the rat race without becoming a rat.

While on an American Airlines flight, I was fortunate enough to make the acquaintance of Robert Crandall, chairman and president of American Airlines, who sat just across the aisle. A few months later I called him and shared with him my concept for this book. When I asked him what he thought of a title like *Winning the Rat Race without Becoming a Rat*, I was pleasantly surprised by his response: "It's an excellent title because it represents a very real dilemma. Most of the senior people I know in business would much prefer to avoid decisions that create hardship for individual employees. On the other hand, we all know that, across the long term, if the company doesn't make a profit, the outlook for its employees is very poor."

"From what I've seen, making a profit in the airline industry is no small challenge," I observed.

"We are constantly trying to find ways to reduce our costs, and this is particularly difficult in the airline business because we are very labor-intensive," Crandall replied. "We are constantly trying to make changes in the number of people we use and how we allocate and how we pay them. These are not always pleasant decisions because they adversely affect a certain number of employees. In the long run, however, these decisions protect the interests of most of the employees by trying to make the company profitable. So I understand what you are saying—trying to win the rat race in a very competitive business environment but trying to do it without being a rat. That's a real challenge."

I knew that Crandall was speaking from a very personal and recent experience. In 1993 a flight attendant strike had crippled American temporarily before Crandall acceded to President Clinton's request that the airline accept binding arbitration.

Unless you live congruently with your personal values, you will never be happy. You'll always have that vague feeling that you've been a rat, are a rat, or are about to become a rat.

Bob Crandall is my kind of CEO because he's willing to admit that he struggles with very real problems and challenges. He's willing to confront his strengths and weaknesses as he tries to keep a huge company on course.

If you're going to win in business, you need to know what you do well and where you may need some help. In the next chapter, I'll give you a quick birth order analysis that probably will be, at the very least, surprising, but I'm betting that it will be a lot more than that. As we will see, none of us fall very far from our limb on the family tree, and that family tree has an awful lot to do with how we operate in the business world today.

The Bottom Line

1. How important to me is dealing with people according to how they view life? How do my actions prove that I am constantly aware of the need to do this?

2. Am I winning the rat race without becoming a rat? Do I really believe I can practice the Golden Rule in business and still win?

3. Do I really believe that what I do is a service to other people? On a scale of one (not much) to ten (a great deal), how committed am I to the proposition that there is more to making money than making money?

4. Am I successful? Am I happy? How do I know?

CHAPTER TWO

It's 10:00 P.M....
Do You Know What Birth Order
Your Accountant Is?

The first time I met T. Boone Pickens, billionaire oil magnate, we were on the same TV talk show pushing books we had just written. As we sat in the greenroom waiting to go on, he saw me holding a copy of *The Birth Order Book*.

"What's birth order?" Boone wanted to know.

Since walking in I had been watching Boone and I thought I'd take a shot at guessing his birth order: "Well, you're probably an only child, aren't you?"

Boone looked at me rather strangely and said, "Why, yes, have we met?"

"No. I'm Dr. Kevin Leman. I'm a psychologist and birth order is something I use in my work."

We started talking about birth order and, after ten minutes of my instruction, Boone was suggesting uses for birth order I'd never thought of, and I'm the guy who supposedly wrote the book!

A typical only child, Boone has a mind like the proverbial steel trap. He travels with his wife, Bea, and an entourage of several other people, but something occurred that day that had never happened before, or since, for that matter. Boone went on first and, after his six-minute spot on the show, everyone got up and

*Y*ou know, this makes sense. Big business and industry would be smart to pay attention to everyone's birth order, I would think—especially when assigning certain jobs within the organization.
—*T. Boone Pickens*

was ready to board the limo and head for the airport. But this time Boone said, "Everybody sit down. Dr. Leman's on next, and we're going to learn something about birth order."

When I finished with my segment, Boone said something I'll never forget. In fact, I remember it as though it were yesterday: "You know, this makes sense. Big business and industry would be smart to pay attention to everyone's birth order, I would think—especially when assigning certain jobs within the organization."

Needless to say, my encounter with T. Boone Pickens made my day and then some. In a few minutes, he had grasped what I had been trying to tell people for over twenty years. The first person you want to understand completely is *you*—how you operate the best, who you operate the best with, and how to use your strengths and shore up your weaknesses. I like to put it this way:

LEMAN'S LAW #2:

**Know self first,
then stick nose in the business of others.**

Birth Orders Come in Three Basic Sizes

To know yourself, you need to understand your own birth order. Many decades ago Alfred Adler, a psychiatrist, pioneered in the theory of birth order and developed a system that says we all fall into one of three basic categories:

First borns—who are known for being capable, conscientious, hard-driving, perfectionistic, exacting, logical, scholarly, and organized. They don't like surprises and because many of them are so aggressive, they are often labeled "Type A personalities." But not all first borns are automatically aggressive. Some are very compliant, although they still possess many of the traits already mentioned.

Middle children—who are born between the first and last in families of three or more. From birth, middles are squeezed by the ones above and the ones below. They learn a lot about negotiating, mediating, and compromising. They also tend to be very social and friends are very important to them.

Last borns—or babies of the family—who are often "people persons" because they have had to learn how to get along with those siblings above them in order to survive. Their experience with all those big brothers and sisters at home has equipped them to know how to persuade, coax, and charm others to get them to do what they want them to do. Engaging, uncomplicated attention-getters, last borns are often family clowns or comedians. Last borns usually grow up feeling special because they mark the end of the family trail.

In this chapter and the next, I'll be describing how the three basic birth orders match up and combine in the world of business. Obviously, I can't go into exhaustive detail. It would take an extra book to do that, and it's available (*The Birth Order Book*, Dell Publishing, 1987).

What I want to do here, however, is highlight some typical strengths and weaknesses of each birth order *as they pertain to business*. Keep in mind as you read that not every strength or weakness may apply to you. No person has *all* the "typical" characteristics attributed to his or her birth order. Each of us is a unique blend of characteristics and personality traits that are caused by different factors (genetics, for example) and birth order is only one of them.

My goal in describing these typical strengths and weaknesses of each birth order is to get you acquainted with the typical birth order traits I have seen and identified in over twenty years of counseling and consulting. At the same time, you can start identifying areas you need to think about and work on regarding how you operate in the business rat race on a daily basis. Also, always keep in mind:

LEMAN'S LAW #3:

Whatever your birth order, your strength is probably your weakness.

Strengths and Weaknesses of First Borns

Never were the words, "Your strength is your weakness" truer spoken than of the first born. For example, if you are the typically assertive, aggressive first born, leadership probably comes easily and naturally. People appreciate your ability to take charge and know what to do. You command respect and find it easy to get people to follow your unflinching leadership. You are probably known for your promise, "I'll take care of it," and your ability to back the statement up.

But the other side of that coin is that you can undermine the initiative of those who lean on you too much. And in your haste to lead your followers where you want to go, you may run roughshod over them and others. You may be so focused on your goals that you don't appreciate the feelings of others and you may come off as insensitive, selfish, too demanding, overbearing, and even arrogant.

Another typical trait of the aggressive first born is to be driven and the strengths that come out of that are that you are ambitious, enterprising, and energetic. You are willing to sacrifice to be a success. You can put in the extra hours, go the extra steps, or even the extra miles to get the job done, and people notice this.

On the downside, however, that strength can turn into a weakness if your workaholic ways put your colleagues under too much pressure. If you're finding it difficult to get people to team up with you at work, you might want to check just how driven you are. If your fellow workers could tell you the truth, perhaps what they'd like to say is, "Lighten up," or "Slow down—I just don't want to run that fast!"

If you're a first born and finding it difficult to get people to team up with you at work, you might want to check just how driven you are. If your fellow workers could tell you the truth, perhaps what they'd like to say is, "Lighten up," or "Slow down—I just don't want to run that fast!"

Winner at Work, Rat at Home?

Right here is as good a spot as any to remind first borns (and all the other birth orders, as well), that the very traits or abilities that enable you to succeed at work can lead to having things fall apart at home. I don't think it's any coincidence that Lee Iacocca, one of the most capable CEOs who ever lived, has had three divorces. Nor is it any coincidence that the talk-show host, Larry King, whose guests are almost always among the movers and shakers of this world, has also been divorced several times.

The fact is, success down at the office or the plant doesn't

*T*he fact is, success down at the office or the plant doesn't always suggest that you're a success at home. Too often, exactly the opposite is the case.

always suggest that you're a success at home. Too often, exactly the opposite is the case.

When I interviewed Robert Crandall, chairman and president of American Airlines, I asked him what he thought of the maxim "Put your spouse first." His response: "Yes, that's true. On the other hand, you have to have a spouse who recognizes that the number of times she can ask to be first is limited." Crandall also went on to say that putting your spouse first doesn't have much to do with business, that it's more of a "personal value set" than a "business value set."

There, of course, is the rub—trying to separate business from the family almost completely. When this happens, it's usually the family that gets the short end of the stick.

No One Can Fill Your Shoes at Home

I was once speaking to a group of wives whose husbands were members of a highly demanding organization that required sixty-hour-plus weeks of their people. After finishing my talk, which had included many suggestions that men ought to be home more and doing more around the house, I opened the session for questions. I had noticed that a few husbands were also present, and one very authoritative looking gentleman rose to his feet and let me know that I didn't understand his organization. When a woman married into this organization, she knew from Day One the organization had to come first.

I let the gentleman rant and rave for a little while longer, then I interrupted by saying, "Excuse me, sir, I really do believe I understand what you're saying about your organization. But the fact is, if you died tonight, they would have someone filling your shoes by 9:00 A.M. tomorrow."

As the gentleman wilted back into his seat, I got a standing ovation from the wives in the room. He had provided a perfect illustration of the point I was making. The job is *not* everything. No matter what position you hold—CEO on down—that position can be filled by somebody else, often by the next morning. At home, this isn't the case. When you take on the commitment of marriage and parenting, *no one can fill your shoes at home*. While you're off winning the rat race, you're leaving a gap at home that no one else can bridge. And when the gap gets too large, you become a rat.

Another way to put it is that, if you're not careful, your job can become a tyrant. We're all familiar with the "tyranny of the urgent." Many a man—and in recent years the women are joining in—has spent his life taking care of urgent business at the office while the important things at home went untended.

While I was on a recent United Airlines flight, the captain came out of the cockpit and came down the aisle greeting some of the passengers. As he came to me I asked, "How's the first-born captain doing today?"

"Have we met?" he asked, looking at me strangely.

"No, but you *are* a first born, aren't you?" (I was pretty sure of my ground. Most airline pilots are first borns, and I've even done a survey to prove it—see Chapter Seven.)

"Well, yes, I am," he said, and we got into a conversation. In less than five minutes he was telling me about his third wife serving him with divorce papers as the tears rolled down his cheeks. He was a successful captain of an airliner, one of the best in his business and in a high-stress position, but at home he had crashed three times. The bottom line here is simple:

LEMAN'S LAW #4:

The urgent is the mortal enemy of the important.

Not All First Borns Are Aggressive

Now it's possible that you're a first born who has been reading my little sermon on workaholism and wondering where you fit in because you're laid back, relaxed, and anything but an aggressive, Type A sort. On the *Parent Talk* radio show that I cohost daily, we average two or three calls a week from moms or dads who want to know what's wrong with their first-born son or daughter. They aren't achieving, they aren't even trying. They seem to have given up. What's going on?

My first answer is always the same: Many first borns respond to their two big role models, mom and dad, by becoming passive and compliant—especially if mom or dad is a critical perfectionist. The constant criticism from parents can wear down some first borns and they go into a shell, so to speak. It's better not to try because it seems safer.

But there is another kind of compliant first born. He or she is the quiet one who learns that it is easier to avoid failure and find success by always being cooperative and easy to work with. The compliant "follower type" first borns meet their need for approval by being the ones who can always be counted on to get done whatever needs doing.

There's a lot to be said for the compliant first borns in business. Middle manager, secretary, and administrative assistant are just a few of many positions where they can excel. The problem is, in the business world, they're out there swimming with the sharks, as Harvey Mackay would put it, and sometimes they can be eaten alive if they're not careful.

So, if you're a first born who leans toward being more compliant than aggressive, beware of being taken advantage of, bullied, or bluffed. Learn to speak up.

I recall counseling Malcolm, a compliant first born, who was being ignored at work and steam-rollered at home by his super-aggressive only-child wife, who was much quicker on the verbal trigger than he was. I advised him to start speaking up at home and at work because he was basically intelligent, logical, and had many good ideas.

If you're a first born who leans toward being more compliant than aggressive, beware of being taken advantage of, bullied, or bluffed. Learn to speak up.

A week or two later, Malcolm came back to see me and told of being in a meeting where he was sitting there bored with everyone's wrangling over a rather simple problem. He had gotten fed up with the rest of the staff as they chased their tails and had finally said, "Excuse me, I'm wondering if it wouldn't be a good idea to look at the problem this way. What we *could* do is . . ." And then he laid out a simple but excellent solution to the problem that had been baffling the entire staff.

Everyone in the room sat there stunned. The sphinx had finally spoken and from his lips had come exactly what they needed! Malcolm's boss was particularly pleased, and after the meeting he stopped him to say, "Malcolm, I was impressed by your contributions in there today. I hope that we'll be hearing more from you."

First Borns Avoid Failure Like the Plague

If you're a typical first born, you have been programmed for success from Day One. You pride yourself in being a perfectionist who leaves no stone unturned to do a thorough job. Even when you were just a few months old, you started trying to avoid something that you simply could not accept—*failure.* Why? Because two all-powerful perfect beings who never made mistakes—your parents—were your only role models.

It's no wonder, then, that first borns are typically careful, cautious, law-abiding folk. As I see the little first born cautiously going through life, it reminds me of someone wading out into a lake with an unfamiliar bottom. He will inch his way along, in crablike fashion, feeling for the drop-off he suspects may be just a few inches away.

Because they are so cautious and careful, first borns wind up in professions that require these traits. I recall traveling to the fair state of Ohio to speak to the Ohio Society of Accountants. I got up to the podium and looked back at exactly 221 accountants, many of whom were giving me a baleful stare and glancing at their watches. I decided it was time for everyone to loosen up a bit, so I said, "Will all of you first borns and only children please rise."

Even I was surprised at how many people got up—practically the entire room! Next I asked those who hadn't stood to stand now. We counted nineteen accountants who weren't first borns or only children, and then I asked the nineteen middle children and last borns one more simple question: "What are you doing *here*?" The room roared with laughter, and if the evening would have ended right there, I would have felt it was a success. It isn't often that you can get over two hundred accountants to smile, much less guffaw out loud.

The point is, accountants take their jobs very seriously. Often the success of a company will rise or fall based upon how careful a bean counter you have. Harvey Mackay believes that the first person you want to hire (after yourself) is a good accountant.[1] And, I might add, be sure he or she is a first born.

Once your first-born accountant is in place, the rest should be easy.

Life Is Never Perfect for Perfectionists

But there is a dark side to perfectionism. For one thing, you may tend to be far too critical. You beat yourself up, as well as those around you, as you constantly find every flaw within forty yards and beyond. You may tend never to be satisfied, and you're never able to quite finish a job because there is always "something more" that should be done.

I have counseled many clients who are perfectionists. . . . My advice is always the same: "Flaunt your imperfections. Try making a few mistakes."

Or, you may have a hard time getting started on a job. It seems odd to think that a perfectionist would be a procrastinator, but that's exactly what happens in many cases because as you think how perfectly you want to do something, you keep putting it off. Why? Because you fear you cannot do it well enough.

I have counseled many clients who are perfectionists. Usually they come to me because they are driving their spouse and/or their children nuts, and they realize it. In most cases, they were set up to be perfectionists themselves by critical parents. My advice is always the same: "Flaunt your imperfections. Try making a few mistakes."

They look at me incredulously. How can they possibly do this? I tell them, "Do this, or you will destroy yourself and your loved ones."

So deadly is the disease of perfectionism that I strongly prescribe learning to be a seeker of excellence, not a perfectionist. There is the real possibility that if you continue to be a compulsive flaw-picker, you may be standing in one of the employment lines, résumé in hand, wondering why those "incompetent fools" let you go. More on this in Chapter Eight.

Harvey Mackay's Secret to Success

I **pride myself on having a fanatical attention to detail. I prepare to win. I'm a fanatic for doing my homework, for doing my research, for being resourceful. I'm always overprepared. You just can't do enough preparation.**
—*Harvey Mackay,*
Chairman and CEO, Mackay
Envelope Corporation

Two more first-born strengths that go together nicely are being logical and scholarly. If you're a logical first born, you're probably known for being a straight thinker who can be counted on not to be compulsive or to go off half-cocked. That's all to the good, but be careful. You may slip into thinking that you're *always* right and fail to pay enough attention to the more intuitive opinions of others, particularly the last-born babies who fly by the seat of their pants. If you work with a last born who is driving you a bit nuts, be aware that you don't think alike, but that doesn't mean the last born's opinions aren't valid.

And if you're scholarly, you're probably a voracious reader. You love to accumulate information and facts, which you use to be an excellent problem solver who thinks things through. Again, be careful. Sometimes gathering facts and information goes under the very official and even intriguing title of "research." You can spend too much time doing research when there are other things that need to be done.

The ideal balance is to gather enough details and facts and then move on them. A first born who obviously has been able to do this very well is Harvey Mackay, whose three best-sellers, totaling seven million books, have been sold in eighty countries and translated into thirty-five languages throughout the world. As

I talked with Harvey, I commented, "I don't know a thing about your personal life, but I would guess you're the only son or first-born son in the family."

"Well, I've got a sister three years older," Harvey replied.

I wasn't surprised. Read Harvey Mackay's books and you will find phrases such as, "Analyze your competition," "Measure your results," and "Draw up a plan." As we had begun our conversation, one of the first things I noticed about Harvey was that he has a need to know. As he peppered me with questions, he seemed to be saying, "Hey, I need to know the details. I don't get going until I know the details; you've got to give me the details."

When I mentioned his strong need for information, Harvey responded with good advice from a first born to anyone who wants to win in business:

"I pride myself on having a fanatical attention to detail. I prepare to win. I'm a fanatic for doing my homework, for doing my research, for being resourceful. I'm always overprepared. You just can't do enough preparation."

Only Children Are Super First Borns

Prepared, organized, hardworking, aggressive, bossy, perfectionistic—all these and more apply to first borns and, I might add, to only children who are super first borns and then some. If you're an only child, the important question is *why* you were an only. There are usually two basic possibilities:

1. Your parents planned for only one child and they stuck with the plan. This usually means that you had a very tightly structured, highly disciplined upbringing, always being pressed to be grown up, responsible, and dependable.

I've counseled many only children who appeared very cool and calm on the surface, but just underneath they were seething with inner rebellion. All their lives they had resented having to be little adults, and now that they had reached adulthood, they were finally kicking over the traces in one way or another.

2. The other typical reason that you are an only child is that your parents could have only one, and all their energy and attention (and a certain amount of spoiling) got poured into their "special jewel." You were the center of the universe for your parents as you grew up. In fact, those feelings of specialness that you enjoyed could have given you some strong baby-of-the-family traits.

At any rate, it's a good bet you were probably sheltered and kept from reality in your earlier years. You may have developed a typical trait of many only children—a certain amount of feeling overly important. Now that you've reached adulthood, you may cope with what could be a lifelong problem—being self-centered, because it's hard to break that pattern molded long ago by Mom and Dad.

Don't take the self-centered label too hard. Keep in mind that an only child never has to face the reality of learning how to share with little brothers and sisters. It's natural enough to feel overly important. Now that you've gone out into the world, you may find times when things don't go your way and you are often tempted to twist that inbred feeling of overimportance into thinking you're being treated unfairly.

Alfred Adler Was Wrong About Onlies

Until recent years, only children were given a bad rap by just about everyone, including Alfred Adler, a psychology pioneer and the "father of birth order." Adler's quote on only children is infamous, but also extremely inaccurate and bordering on slander. One day, evidently after having had a close encounter of an unpleasant kind with an only child, Alfie said: "The only child has difficulties with every independent activity and sooner or later they become useless in life."[2]

Obviously, there have been plenty of only children who would make Dr. Adler eat his words. From Franklin D. Roosevelt to Ted Koppel and Dr. James Dobson; from Lena Horne, Lauren Bacall, and Brooke Shields to Roger Staubach and Joe Montana; only children have achieved in just about every area, and that includes business.

I've already introduced you to T. Boone Pickens, the oil tycoon who built Mesa Petroleum into America's largest oil company worth close to three billion dollars at one time. I also recently learned that Robert E. Allen, CEO of AT&T, is also an only child. Another only child at the top of the business ladder is Carl Icahn, architect of some of the biggest corporate takeovers in history, including Phillips Petroleum and TWA. Among Icahn's legendary achievements was purchasing and later selling a huge chunk of Texaco stock, resulting in the largest single trade in the history of the New York Stock Exchange at a profit of more than five hundred million, including dividends.

One Wall Street observer commented:

Carl is a one-man operation. He doesn't really need a lawyer. He doesn't need advisors. He has a great grasp of everything himself. All the issues, legal or business, he sees each one and how they interrelate. And most impressive, he sees them all instantaneously.[3]

Only children like Pickens, Allen, and Icahn are good reasons to realize it's never a good idea to stereotype any particular birth order and put someone in a certain slot or rut because of what you've heard or read. Obviously, some only children might come out "spoiled, selfish, lazy, aloof, and lonely." But I've known middle children and last borns who fit these categories, too.

There are plenty of only children who have all the first-born pluses and strengths discussed in this chapter and more. And they have used them well in the workplace. The well-adjusted only child whose parents haven't spoiled him rotten will quite typically have great initiative, good self-esteem, and never have felt all that lonely either.[4]

On that note we'll wrap up the strengths and weaknesses of first borns and only children. With all that ability and natural leadership, it almost sounds as though they might dominate the business world. In the next chapter, as we look at middle children and last-born babies, a key truth will be evident. All birth orders have their strengths and weaknesses. All birth orders have advantages and disadvantages in the business rat race. What each birth order must learn is how to compete—and blend—with the others.

The Bottom Line

1. Do I drive myself and those I work with too hard? What would my fellow workers say?

2. Am I a workaholic? In other words, is work more important than *everything* or *everyone* else?

3. Am I a winner at work and a rat at home? What would my spouse and children say?

4. If I'm a compliant first born, do I need to speak up and make my opinions known? What steps can I take to do this?

5. Am I afraid of failure? Do I learn from failure, or does it get me down?

Strengths and Weaknesses of First-Born or Only Children That Can Affect Their Business Performance

Typical Traits	Strengths	Weaknesses
Leaders	Take charge, know what to do.	May undermine the initiative of those who lean on them too much; or may come off as too overbearing or aggressive.
If aggressive	Command respect, others want to follow their unflinching leadership.	Can run roughshod over others, may be insensitive and tend to be selfish, too focused on the goal and not enough on the feelings of others.
If compliant	Cooperative, easy to work with, good team players.	Can be taken advantage of, bullied, bluffed.
Perfectionistic	Always do things right, leave no stone unturned to do a thorough job.	Tend to criticize themselves and/or others too much. Never satisfied, may procrastinate because they fear they cannot do a "good enough job."
Organized	Have everything under control, always on top of things; tend to be on time and on schedule.	May worry too much about order, process, and rules and not be flexible when it's needed. May show real impatience with anyone who is "disorganized" or not as meticulous.
Drivers	Ambitious, enterprising, energetic; willing to sacrifice to be a success.	Put themselves or those they work with under too much stress and pressure.
List makers	They set goals and reach them; they tend to get more done in a day.	May become boxed in, too busy with the to-do list to see the big picture and what needs to be done right now, or later.
Logical	Known as straight thinkers, can be counted on not to be compulsive or to go off half-cocked.	May believe they're always right and fail to pay attention to the more intuitive opinions of others.
Scholarly	Tend to be voracious readers, accumulators of information and facts; good problem solvers who think things through.	May spend too much time gathering facts when there are other things that need to be done; may be so serious they fail to see the humor in situations when humor is desperately needed.

CHAPTER THREE

Need to Cut a Deal or Make a Sale? Call a Later Born—Fast!

I f you are a later born in your family, all this talk about first-born leadership initiative and ability may have been a little intimidating. You may be wondering if there is any hope for later borns making their mark in the business world. You may fear you have to run the rat race with a handicap because those first borns got out of the blocks a lot sooner!

Not to worry. As you will see, middle children and last borns have gifts that some first borns would kill for—figuratively speaking, of course. More often than not, the entrepreneurs of this world are middle children. More often than not, the best sales people are babies of their families. There is something about being born later that gives you an edge, especially with people. You are far more likely to be a good negotiator, mediator, and deal maker. You are far more likely to be skilled in reading other people, knowing how they feel and how to make them feel good— even make them laugh and enjoy themselves.

Yes, if you're later born, you have a lot going for you, and keep in mind that you have been relieved of that toughest of all jobs on this earth: growing up first born in the family and enduring all that pressure, all that experimentation by parents who didn't quite know what they were doing but knew they wanted their first born to "do it right."

In a way, you owe first borns a big debt of gratitude. They ran interference for you, took a lot of the flak and all those lectures that began: "You're the *oldest*—I expected *more* out of you than that!" You escaped those haunting feelings that everyone depended on you; that you couldn't get away with anything; that you never were allowed to be a child; that if you didn't do it, it wouldn't get done.

*Y*ou have your strengths and weaknesses— everybody does. But don't think for a minute that to be born later means to be born less.

That first-born big brother or big sister snowplowed the road of life for you in a very real way. He or she made it possible for you to be a kid. He or she is the one who became your role model and because that first-born big brother or sister was far less than perfect, you probably escaped that curse called perfectionism that so many first borns inherit from having mom and dad as their role models in the early years of life.

So, if you're a later born, celebrate! There are places for you in the world of business that no first born can fill. Of course, you have your strengths and weaknesses—everybody does. But don't think for a minute that to be born later means to be born less. It just ain't so, and in this chapter I'll explain why.

Strengths and Weaknesses of Middle Children

If you are a middle child—in other words, you weren't born first and you weren't born last—it may or may not comfort you to know you are the hardest birth order to analyze and the most unpredictable. I liken you middle children to the quail who nicely blend into the desert here in our suburban backyard in Tucson. The reason for this is that you develop your style of operating in life with two things working for you—or against you, as the case may be.

First, as the one in the middle, you probably grew up feeling squeezed—from above and below. I've counseled with many a middle child who let me know that he or she didn't feel all that special while growing up. The first born got all the attention and glory while the baby got away with murder.

The other important element in your development was what we call the "branching off effect." A reason that it is so hard to predict how a middle child will come out is that the middle child is always playing off the first born above him. Generally speaking, all the research studies done on birth order show that second borns are quite likely to be somewhat the opposite of first borns. That's why middle children can take such different directions.

The middle child can wind up a quiet shy loner or a very friendly outgoing social lion. He or she may be impatient, easily frustrated, or able to take life in stride. The middle child can wind up the family rebel or goat or can play the role of peacemaker and mediator in the family. The middle child may be a competitive scrapper or he may choose to be easygoing and avoid conflict. After years of counseling, I have concluded:

LEMAN'S LAW #5:

**The middle child is
a mixed bag of talents and abilities.**

Donald Trump: Aggressive Deal Maker

Donald Trump, the real estate wheeler-dealer who soared to the top in the '80s, crashed in the early '90s, and then started to make a comeback by the mid-'90s,[1] is a prime example of a middle child who took the aggressive route. As the fourth born of five, Donald looked above at two older sisters and a first-born big brother, Freddy, Jr. As the first-born boy in the family, Freddy, Jr., was being groomed to follow in his dad's footsteps and become

*A*s a middle child, you above all others are willing to know yourself a lot better because you've seen life from a more realistic standpoint. Nothing was ever easy.

a hard-driving builder and manager of huge apartment buildings in New York City.

The only problem was that Freddy, Jr., turned out to be a complacent, compliant boy—someone who wanted to please people rather than control them or run roughshod over them. As the Trump children grew into adulthood, Donald, eight years younger than Freddy, did a "role reversal" on his older brother more or less by default.

Instead of buckling down to the real estate business, Freddy went off to fly airplanes, even becoming a professional pilot who flew for TWA. He also loved fishing and boating, but he never loved real estate, and Donald used to tell him, "C'mon, Freddy, what are you doing? You're wasting your time."

Trump admits in his autobiography that he later regretted ever having uttered things like that, and he went on to say: "Along the way, I think Freddy became discouraged, and he started to drink, and that led to a downward spiral. At the age of forty-three, he died. It's very sad, because he was a wonderful guy who never quite found himself. In many ways he had it all, but the pressures of our particular family were not for him. I only wished I had realized this sooner."[2]

As I describe some of the basic strengths that can be found in many middle children, you may or may not fit, but where the shoe does fit, take some careful notes. As a middle child, you above all others are willing to know yourself a lot better because you've seen life from a more realistic standpoint. Nothing was ever easy. You had to negotiate for everything. At least one sibling above you told you how to run your life and someone below you got all the attention for doing even the simplest things while you went unnoticed.

Middle Children Are Typically Entrepreneurs

There is at least one research study whose results show that entrepreneurs are most likely to come from the middle rather than the top or the bottom of the family. Middle children are far more apt to take a risk than their cautious first-born siblings, and when they take those risks they are far more capable than the babies of the family in mediating and negotiating them to a successful conclusion. Babies of the family may love to make sales, but middle children have the patience and staying power to make deals and see them through. That's why they stand out as entre-preneurs.

Donald Trump, one of the more flamboyant wheeler-dealers of the twentieth century, put it this way: "I don't do it for the money. I've got enough, much more than I'll ever need. I do it to do it. Deals are my art form. Other people paint beautifully on canvas or write wonderful poetry. I like to make deals, preferably big deals. That's how I get my kicks."[3]

If you have these entrepreneurial traits, one reason is that you have an independent streak that came out of feeling squeezed at home. A well-known theory says that all of us operate with three natural motivations: one, to obtain rewards and recognition; two, to avoid pain and danger; three, to get even.[4] The middle child is a little different, because he's *often* "getting even." That explains his free spirit and why he often winds up trying to start a business for himself.

I once counseled a couple where the husband was a middle child and the wife constantly complained that he was a noncom-municating, independent character who never let her really get close. When I talked with him, I learned that he operated at home in exactly the same way he operated at work, where he was an assistant manager in a men's clothing store. He got along well enough with the people he supervised, but he still ran things his way, "because I know what's really needed." Not surprisingly, he left that job to start his own business, which became quite successful.

If you are the independent entrepreneur, you may well be in business for yourself or you may want to be. As an independent thinker, you may be known among your fellow employees as willing to do things differently, take risks, and strike out in your own direction. This can be good as long as they don't perceive you as appearing to be bullheaded, stubborn, or unwilling to cooperate.

If You're a Social Lion, Don't Roar Too Loudly

*N*ot all typical traits of a particular birth order apply to any individual. We're all unique blends of different skills and characteristics.

If you're a friendly, team player–type of middle child, you've obviously avoided overdoing any independent streak, if you have one at all. Remember, *not all typical traits of a particular birth order apply to any individual.* We're all unique blends of different skills and characteristics. The challenge is to recognize the traits and characteristics that are yours and learn how to make the most of them.

If you have picked up the middle-child ability to make friends easily, this is obviously a tremendous asset in your business life, particularly if you are in sales (see Chapters Four, Five, and Six).

But even here there is a danger. Because you grew up wanting friends, needing friends, and finally going out first from your family to find friends, it could well be that relationships are *too* important to you. You simply can't risk offending a friend, and in business this can cloud your judgment and cause you to make extremely unwise decisions.

If you suspect you might be guilty of letting certain relationships affect your work, find a trusted friend or mentor who can level with you on what he sees you doing and perhaps help you work your way out of any corners you've painted yourself into.

If You're Good at "Working Things Out"

From their earliest years, middle children are used to stepping into the middle to make peace, carry messages, and work things out. Their motivation is simple. They can't get their way with the first-born birthright or last-born manipulation, so they learn the art of give-and-take, negotiation, and compromise.

These are all invaluable skills in the business arena, whether refereeing a disagreement between two employees or negotiating an important contract.

One pair of specialists in the business field believe that next to reading and writing, negotiation is the most important skill to learn if you want to be successful. Instead of settling for what you've been given, you can use negotiation as a tool to get what you want. In their book, *The Total Negotiator*, Stephen Pollan and Mark Levine describe negotiators as proactive people who "never willingly settle for less than what they want. Negotiators don't accept things as they are without first asking why they couldn't be made better. Negotiators go after what they want."[5]

If you're too compromising . . . the sharks will smell blood and will move in to take advantage of you—or for the kill.

Middle children are often good mediators because they've grown up settling things between their siblings. They've also learned the art of diplomacy and compromise, which can be useful tools in the business community. If you're a middle child, however, keep in mind that you should guard against failing to share your real feelings about a project, a decision, or perhaps a certain person in a key position. Your lack of candor can be seen as a real weakness, even a handicap in certain situations.

The point is, you are good at the art of compromise, and that's why you could be skilled at mediating disputes or negotiating disagreements. But watch the downside of that as well: If you're too compromising, you can be seen as willing to have peace at any price. The sharks will smell blood and will move in to take advantage of you—or for the kill.

Strengths and Weaknesses of Middle Children That Can Affect Their Business Performance

Typical Traits	Strengths	Weaknesses
Reasonable expectations	Because life hasn't always been fair, you are unspoiled, realistic.	Being treated unfairly may have made you suspicious, cynical, even bitter.
Social lion	Relationships are very important; you make friends and tend to keep them.	Friends can be too important and not offending them may cloud your judgment on key decisions.
Independent thinker	Willing to do it differently, take a risk, strike out on your own.	You may appear to be bullheaded, stubborn, unwilling to cooperate.
Compromising	You know how to get along with others, can be skilled at mediating disputes or negotiating disagreements.	You can be seen as willing to have peace at any price and others may try to take advantage of you.
Diplomatic	You are a peacemaker, willing to work things out.	You may hate confrontation and often choose not to share your real opinions and feelings.
Secretive	You can be trusted with sensitive information; you keep your mouth shut.	You may fail to admit it when you need help—it's just too embarrassing.

You Already Know "Life Isn't Fair"

If there is one birth order who doesn't have to be told "Life isn't fair," it's the middle children. If you came through the slings and arrows of childhood in good shape, you have turned the unfairness of life into a strength. You don't have unreasonable expectations and you are unspoiled, yet realistic.

On the other hand, being treated unfairly may have made you a bit cynical or suspicious of others. If you have really gotten a bad deal, you may be downright bitter and rebellious.

But even though life didn't seem quite fair to a lot of middle children, as you take stock as an adult you may look back and see that there are real advantages. One client once told me, ". . . as an adult I really believe I can cope with problems better because I got a lot of good training in give-and-take while I was growing up."[6]

That's not a bad way to look at it. Donald Trump, the entrepreneur who climbed so high and then fell so far, has this to add. It's good advice for all of us from a middle child who seems to know himself quite well:

> I don't kid myself. Life is very fragile, and success doesn't change that. If anything, success makes it more fragile. Anything can change, without warning, and that's why I try not to take any of what's happened too seriously. Money was never a big motivation for me, except as a way to keep score. The real excitement is playing the game. I don't spend a lot of time worrying about what I should have done differently, or what's going to happen next. If you ask me exactly what the deals . . . all add up to in the end, I'm not sure I have a very good answer. Except that I've had a very good time making them.[7]

Strengths and Weaknesses of Last Borns

As I began work on this book, I decided it was time to buy a new car. After looking in vain at some "hot items" recommended by friends, I decided to go back to the dealership where I had bought my Chrysler several years and about one hundred thousand miles earlier. As I drove in, I noticed a brand-new green Sebring convertible sitting out in front at the far end of the front row. Next I spotted the sales manager whom I had dealt with before. All I asked was, "The green convertible in the front row. Does it have leather seats and all the other goodies?"

In fifteen minutes we had a deal. My sales manager friend knew what I would pay for a car, and I made it clear I wanted to buy that car *today*. He didn't go down without a fight, but he knew I meant it when I made my "three hundred dollars over invoice" offer. Finally, he gave in. I didn't even test-drive the car; I just signed the papers and drove it home.

As I took my first-born wife, Sande, to the driveway to show her my new car, I began to have second thoughts. What if Baby Cub had blown it and the green convertible was really bilious chartreuse? After all, I'm color blind.

Sande took one look and cooed, "Oh, Leemy, I *love* it!" As I stood there smiling, proud of my taste in cars and my ability to get a good deal, Mama Bear brought the Cub back to earth by adding, "Except the gold colored wheels *are* a *little* tacky."

Why Last Borns Are Impatient and Impetuous

I don't share the green convertible story as an example of how to buy a car (there are many good books that can do that). But it does illustrate two key characteristics of many last borns: impetuousness and impatience. As I pointed out earlier, first borns will study a decision from every angle, reading *Consumer Report* from cover to cover, and then sleep on it before making a final choice. But your typical last born has places to go and people to see. He can't be bothered with all that.

And where does this impatience and impetuousness come

from? All their lives last borns are looked on as the smallest, the weakest, the ones who "don't know how to do that yet." Babies of the family just aren't taken very seriously because, after all, they're too little or too young to be expected to do much right. Even if a last born is lucky enough to have parents who have more sense than to always be putting him down, he isn't likely to escape the slings and arrows tossed his way by his older brothers and sisters, who tend to write him off at every turn as they exert their "superiority" in obvious or subtle ways.

> *Growing up last born can make you a bundle of ambivalence. You may be charming and entertaining one minute, temperamental and rebellious the next.*

It's no wonder, then, that last borns go through life muttering, "I'll show them!" They will show their older brothers and sisters, their parents, and even the world that they are to be reckoned with.

So while last borns may play the role of Crown Prince or Princess—cuddly, spoiled, always good for some laughs and being the center of attention—underneath it all they want to be taken seriously—very seriously, indeed.

In many ways, growing up last born can make you a bundle of ambivalence. You may be charming and entertaining one minute, temperamental and rebellious the next. Last borns who succeed in business have learned to cover that dark side and show the world what they can do in positive and productive ways.

Be Charming but Not "Too Slick"

If you're a typical last born, people see you as charming, attractive, winning, and likable. This is a great strength in that you're easy to talk to. You make things interesting. In short, you're fun. You got all those qualities by spending your entire life learning how to "read" the people around you. First it was your brothers and sisters and, of course, your parents. Then it was friends, teachers, coaches, fellow workers, and bosses.

As you use your charms and winning ways, keep one thing in mind: You can come across as a little "too slick," and that can make you a bit unbelievable—maybe more than a bit unbelievable. And that is the kiss of death in business.

Being People Oriented Has Its Pros and Cons

As a typical baby, you're what I call "people oriented." You thrive in settings where you relate to others. You work well in small groups because you usually don't have a great need to control a situation. You leave that to the first borns.

And if you're a typical last born, you love social settings and like doing business that way. A round of golf with a client is a perfect example.

After all I've said about building relationships, you would think being people oriented is all on the plus side, but it is possible that you may come across as too undisciplined, too prone to talk and not work. Be careful that you don't get labeled as someone who talks a good game but isn't able to put it down on paper or "make it happen."

Be Tenacious but Never Irritating

I've often used my own last-born tenacity to fight my way onto talk shows who turned me down the first few times I called. Obviously, all this persistence goes back to wanting to "show them." I grew up being the clown in my family and in the classroom. Almost every teacher I ever had labeled me "most likely to fail." But once I got to the University of Arizona and started dating Sande, my lovely wife-to-be who played a major role in helping me straighten out my life, I learned how to show the world what I could do in *positive* ways.

The rest is history. Ill equipped as I was to do college-level work (I graduated fourth from the bottom in my high school class), I wouldn't take no for an answer. I got passing grades— even A's. I showed the world and myself I could do it. You may have a similar story. At least you feel you're also the persistent type who simply won't take no as a final word. Use that persistence, but always know when to stop pushing.

There is that point where you can push too hard and where people start reading you as someone who sees things only your way. I really can't emphasize enough the need for last-born babies to curb that natural urge to "show them" by exercising a little wisdom and common sense. Babies must keep in mind:

LEMAN'S LAW #6:

**If you try too hard to "show them,"
they may show you the door!**

Be Lovable but Don't Let Emotions Rule

Because last borns always want strokes themselves, they like to stroke others. They like to reach out to people in an affectionate, engaging way. This is another excellent quality for business, particularly sales, and if you have it, keep polishing your natural aptitudes by always taking time to think things through. In other words, don't make decisions or move impetuously on the basis of emotions. You may think I'm a fine one to talk with the way I buy cars, but as impetuous as it may have seemed, I knew what kind of car I wanted and I didn't have to do a lot of research.

Besides, I don't do all my business that way. When it comes to sizing up speaking opportunities and invitations, for example, I have learned to take my time, sort things out, and give it some thought. I always tell myself, "Leman, you can't help the whole world, so pick your spots carefully."

You May Have Something in Common with Ronald Reagan

Ronald Reagan, fortieth president of the United States, was a baby of the family who was laughed at and criticized by his foes for sometimes acting as if he didn't know what day it was or what was really on the agenda. It's possible in the latter days of his presidency Reagan was already experiencing early symptoms of Alzheimer's disease, with which he was diagnosed later. But for all of that, Reagan had a spontaneous, uncomplicated style. He appeared genuine and trustworthy without a hidden agenda, and this added to his natural charm and ability to communicate with the common voter.

It's my personal opinion that, in many cases, when Reagan came off as not quite knowing what was going on, what we were really seeing was the baby of the family "doing his thing." Underneath, Ronald Reagan knew exactly what was going on and he got the job done as he saw it.

If you have this spontaneous and uncomplicated style, credit it to your baby of the family upbringing, but don't carry it too far. As the baby-of-the-family, you may be remembered as the one who wandered around with your zipper undone or with your underwear in your back pocket. Your motto may have been, "Life is a beach," and Mom's biggest challenge was helping you make sure you didn't show up minus your swim trunks.

So be aware that spontaneity and simplicity can be read by some of the more cynical types as being absentminded, a little off focus, disorganized, or even an "airhead."

Keep That Natural Self-Confidence in Check

Back in the mid-1980s I tried thirteen times to get on the *Donahue Show* to push *The Birth Order Book*. The rejections just kept coming, but I wouldn't give up. Finally, on the fourteenth try I was accepted.

It was one of the first really big talk shows I had ever done, and I'm sure it helped make *The Birth Order Book* a runaway best-seller. I remember the producer calling to say I was on the show and asking, "Will you be nervous? You're *it*; there's nobody else."

I replied, "No problem. In fact, if Phil ever has a day when he doesn't feel good, I'll be glad to sub for him."

When I told the *Donahue* producer that I would be glad to take over for Phil if he ever felt a little ill, was it just last-born egomania talking? Partly. But also involved was the very powerful last-born trait of wanting attention. All kids want attention, but we last borns make a career out of it, and we usually try to get attention by being entertaining and funny.

The obvious downside to wanting all this attention is that you can appear too self-centered. You may come off as someone with a big ego who doesn't want to give others enough credit. So temper your desire to show off or wisecrack, especially at work. Pick your spots carefully and be amusing when it counts—to relieve tension perhaps, or to pep up everybody else in a meeting.

Give It Your Best Shot, Then Go On

As a consummate last born, I have a short story with a moral for any birth order. I do a lot of public speaking, and I've been in a lot of auditoriums where they have a spotlight right in your face. You can hardly see the audience, but you know there are several thousand people out there.

Strengths and Weaknesses of Last Borns That Can Affect Their Business Performance

Typical Traits	Strengths	Weaknesses
Charming	People like you because you're easy to talk to, make things fun and interesting.	You can come across as a "little too slick," perhaps a bit unbelievable.
People oriented	You thrive in business settings where you relate to others. You work well one-on-one or in small groups and you glory in social settings, a round of golf with a client, for example.	You may come across as too undisciplined, too prone to talk and not work. You get labeled as talking a good game but not being able to put it down on paper or make it happen.
Tenacious	You just keep coming with tireless persistence; you won't take no for an answer.	You can push too hard because you see things only your way.
Affectionate, engaging	Because you want strokes yourself, you like to stroke others, to reach out to them.	You could make decisions or move impetuously on the basis of emotions without giving it enough thought.
Uncomplicated	You appear genuine and trustworthy, without a hidden agenda.	You can come off as absentminded or maybe a little off focus.
Attention-seeking	You know how to get noticed, usually by being entertaining or funny.	You can appear too self-centered, with a big ego, unwilling to give others enough credit.

Often, they have mikes out in the audience so people can ask questions at break time. One night I had the misfortune to have a rather unhappy lady get on the mike, and she proceeded to rant and rave for about sixty or seventy seconds about all the things I'd said that she didn't like or agree with. Finally, when she paused for breath, all I said was, "Next!"

The audience broke into spontaneous applause. It was as if the whole auditorium knew that the lady was not interested in giving any constructive criticism. I suppose I could be called rude for simply going on to the next question, but the way I saw it, I had a decision to make and very little time to make it. There was nothing I could do to answer this lady because she really wasn't interested in what I had to say—that was obvious. So rather than let her continue to harpoon me, I just went on to the next person.

A perfectionist might have stumbled around trying to answer this lady's unanswerable questions, but I just didn't feel that was my obligation. Obviously you can attribute that to my being a baby of the family without a perfectionistic bone in my body. I'm willing to give it my best shot, but if it doesn't work or I don't necessarily score points, I shrug it off and go on.

Whatever your birth order, I urge you to do the same. The next time your performance is less than flawless, just tell yourself, "Life is too short to beat myself up when I'm not perfect." Keep telling yourself that, particularly if you suffer from perfectionism (see Chapter Eight). At least you'll be getting practice in knowing yourself and, who knows, there may come a time when one of those flaw-pickers tries to nail you and you'll be able to say, "Next!"

Not only do all birth orders have their strengths and weaknesses, they have their likes and dislikes, their quirks and biases. The better you understand how first borns, middle children, and last borns tick, the more successful you will be in one of the toughest arenas of all—sales.

Somebody said, "Nothing happens until somebody sells something." In the next three chapters we'll look at how a basic knowledge of birth order theory can help you make the contact, make your pitch, and close the sale.

The Bottom Line

1. Which of my strengths could be a weakness? Why? What examples can I think of where one of my strengths turned into a weakness in my business dealings?

2. Am I willing to ask my fellow workers for feedback on my strengths and weaknesses? Who can I ask and in what area will I start?

3. Am I willing to ask my spouse and children for feedback on my strengths and weaknesses? What would they say to me about how much time I spend with the family?

PART II

How a Little Basic Birth Order Will Get You More Orders

When you get right down to it, the sales person who hits the top of the charts is the one who understands human nature the best.

—HARVEY MACKAY

CHAIRMAN AND CEO, MACKAY ENVELOPE
CORPORATION; AUTHOR, *SWIM WITH THE SHARKS
WITHOUT BEING EATEN ALIVE*

CHAPTER FOUR

To See (and Sell) Better, Always Get Behind Your Customer's Eyes

C an a basic knowledge of birth order increase your sales? I'll let Harvey Mackay answer:

. . . when you get right down to it, the salesperson who hits the top of the charts is the one who understands human nature the best.[1]

Early in my counseling career, I wouldn't have understood the wisdom of Harvey Mackay's words. For one thing, I didn't even realize that I, too—a "distinguished psychologist"—was a salesman. Fortunately, my father did.

My father had only an eighth-grade education, but he was successful in raising a family and running his own small dry cleaning business. It's funny, but the older I got, the smarter Dad became. Unfortunately, I had to get quite a bit older—well into my thirties—before I understood his message to be concerned about making sales.

In the early years of my counseling career, Dad would ask, "Kevin, did you have any customers today?"

"Dad," I would protest, "they're not customers, they're *clients*!"

"Do they pay you money?" he wanted to know.

"Yeah, of course they do."

"Then they're customers."

*A*s I counsel, I don't always "make the sale" in trying to get people to change. . . . But that doesn't stop me from learning all I can about them— what I call getting behind their eyes to see the world as they see it.

And, of course, he was right. My dad had a simple intuitive knowledge of human nature. Our practical little conversations eventually helped me realize that my clients were indeed my customers. And once I had that straight, it wasn't much of a stretch to see that what I had learned in my psychology courses, particularly about birth order, could be invaluable. As a counselor, I was basically selling people help—help with their problems, questions, and anxieties. But the more I counseled the more I understood that you can't help people unless you really know them—particularly how they see life.

Fortunately, because of the product I was trying to sell—counseling—I was forced into knowing my customers better and better in order to help them more and more. In fact, I soon learned that after I obtained a client (i.e., customer), I wasn't through making my sale. In fact, I had only begun. The real job lay ahead—selling those I counseled on trying ideas and suggestions to make real changes in their lives.

So as a psychologist, I have constantly been in the business of sales. And that's why I can state the following with confidence:

LEMAN'S LAW #7:

Know your customers, and selling your product will take care of itself.

Obviously, I believe that a working knowledge of birth order is one of the most effective ways to know your customers. Am I saying that birth order will always work and guarantee you a sale?

Of course not. No method *always* works. As I counsel, I don't always "make the sale" in trying to get people to change their dysfunctional and destructive ways. But that doesn't stop me from learning all I can about them—what I call getting behind their eyes to see the world as they see it. *Then* I can sell them what I have to offer—and so can you.

A key to getting behind your customers' eyes is to keep good notes and records on each one. In my business, I do it with the "personal file folder" on each client who comes in for help. I also keep file folders on every organization that requests me for a speaking engagement. When your speaking ability commands five figures, you better know what you're talking about and you also better know *who* you are talking to.

When I am out speaking I am usually taking notes for my files right up to the moment I am introduced. Being a baby of the family, I'm pretty casual about it—often I use a napkin or just a slip of paper, but I jot down what I see in the crowd around me. I take a look at how they are dressed. I listen to the small talk. In the slightest ways I get a feel for what is going to fly with the kind of group I sense in the room.

As you take notes on your customers, it's more likely you will prefer a notebook, or a tool that has grown very popular—the Rolodex. If you can write or print small, perhaps you can pack all the birth order information and other facts on your client right on the Rolodex card. This makes it a handy reference tool when you seek to make another contact that may lead to a potential sale.

No matter how you keep your information on each customer or potential customer, you should continually add to your data whenever you can. You really can't get too much of this personal stuff that helps you understand the people you are dealing with, how they think, their likes and dislikes.

In my own work, I have found personal information on clients

*W*hen meeting a potential client or customer for the first time, the cardinal rule is to never ask anyone for his or her birth order directly. Instead, you want to observe not only how the person looks but what the person says and how the person acts.

especially valuable when dealing with family-owned businesses where I've been called in to solve disagreements or rivalries that are threatening to tear the company apart. When you're trying to sell to a family-owned business, it's good to get behind everyone's eyes to know who's doing the infighting, who's holding the grudge this week, and so on. This can make a big difference in how you service the account or try to get new business.

As you build this gold mine of background on each customer, birth order data can be invaluable. The question is, How do you get it? Now I admit it's not always easy to be sure of a person's birth order but there are signs.

How to Detect Someone's Birth Order

When meeting a potential client or customer for the first time, the cardinal rule is to never ask anyone for his or her birth order directly. Instead, you want to observe not only how the person looks but what the person says and how the person acts.

Signs That Point to First Borns

1. They are typically well dressed, neat, and well groomed from the top of their heads down to their shiny shoes. Keep in mind, however, that being first born and well dressed don't automatically go together. Some first borns wind up "discouraged perfectionists," meaning they can't fulfill their own standards so they don't bother to try (see Chapter Eight). This could translate to their dress, which could be rather sloppy. The

point here is that first borns are usually well groomed and, when you find someone who is a sharp dresser, it's a good bet that you may be dealing with a first born.

2. As they talk, first borns use an impressive vocabulary, but they are more interested in facts than in flash. They constantly bore in on their goals.

3. They are very time conscious and don't have a lot of patience for chitchat. The male first born in particular may wear a digital watch—just to keep more precise track of what time it is.

4. The books in their offices reflect the latest thinking in business practices or other serious subjects related to their jobs. Also, look around for crossword puzzle books among the magazines in the waiting room. First borns love the challenge of solving crosswords because it pays off for their perfectionistic and compulsive thinking. Each puzzle is solved only with the *right* answers, and each puzzle obviously is full of *words*, which first borns love.

*A*s the person talks, listen for words like *extremely* and *very*. First borns are black-and-white thinkers who put strong emphasis into what they say.

5. Their wall hangings and knickknacks reflect a serious philosophical view or commemoration of jobs well done. The telltale signs of a first-born leader who has risen through the ranks are plaques and framed certificates that record significant successes and achievements.

6. Look around the office for any indications of affinity for detail or organization. There may be a carefully grouped montage of pictures or photographs; models of airplanes, antique cars,

or ships may sit on the desk or shelf, carefully constructed down to the very last feature.

Another telltale sign might be one of the many "perpetual motion" machines that are very decorative but show a lot of interest in detail. Also look for supplies that are carefully lined up on desks or shelves.

7. As you interview the person, look for any signs of compulsive behavior—doodling a lot, for example.

8. As the person talks, listen for words like *extremely* and *very*. First borns are black-and-white thinkers who put strong emphasis into what they say. They are analytical and love to ask questions. In Chapter One I mentioned meeting Harvey Mackay over the phone. While I couldn't see him, it wasn't long until I was fairly convinced I was talking to a first born. After ten minutes he was still asking me questions and I was the one who was supposed to be conducting the interview!

Other first-born behavior is the habit of jumping from subject to subject. First borns can be real motormouths whose minds are going a hundred miles an hour.

Signs That Point to Middle Children

1. Middle children are admittedly the toughest to spot, particularly right off the bat. Sometimes you will arrive at believing you are dealing with a middle child by the process of elimination. None of the first-born characteristics described are there in any great degree, nor does this person have any of the typical baby characteristics, such as flamboyancy, being very engaging, fun, and entertaining.

2. As for grooming, middle children won't necessarily look like they're right out of the bandbox, but they won't be sloppy, casual, or flashy in dress either. They are more likely to wear very little jewelry and their clothes tend to be conservative and rather plain. A blue oxford shirt with a button-down collar and a simple blue tie to match are more suggestive of the middle child. Also look for anything that might suggest a "company person"—something pinned to a lapel that mentions the company's name or perhaps a motto or plaque on the wall. Middle children are known for their loyalty to their friends and *to their company*.

*M*iddle children are typically very interested in you. . . . If you find yourself doing a lot of the talking while the other person listens, you are probably dealing with a middle child.

3. Regarding speech and mannerisms, if you're talking with a person who isn't full of emphatic opinions, someone who might say, "You know, I'm not sure about that—let me make a quick call to another department," you're probably dealing with a middle child. First borns, on the other hand, are quick to give you their opinions. Last borns, on the other hand, may not be too interested in answering a question and respond with more of a "Who cares?" attitude.

4. As a rule, a middle child won't have as many books on his or her shelves as a first born. The progressive rule is obvious—only children will have the most books, followed by first borns, and then middle children. Typically, the office with the fewest books will be that of the last born. The earlier born you are, the more apt you are to be a fervent reader; if you're later born, you are likely to read less.

5. Middle children are typically very interested in you—your product, your service, and beyond that, you personally. They are the most likely birth order to ask you about your own family and how things are going for you. If you find yourself doing a lot of the talking while the other person listens, you are probably dealing with a middle child.

6. Middle children love to be team players, so their first response might be to "get some people in here right now to look at this." Their hunger for relationships makes them relational business people.

7. Middle children are the ones who are likely to be down-to-earth—the roll-up-your-sleeves type. If you're calling on someone who has his coat off and who has just finished "eating in" for lunch, you want to make a mental note that this person is likely to be a middle child.

And that's the point about all of these signs or indicators that I have been giving you. You can't see one thing and immediately conclude, "That's it—I've got a middle child on my hands, or a first born, or whatever." What you want to do is keep a mental tally sheet and then write down notes afterward about what you experienced. You may not be able to detect a person's birth order the first time you call, but by observing how he or she behaves you can make a lot of valuable notes that can come in handy as you try to get the person's business in future meetings.

Signs That Point to Last Borns

1. Babies of the family usually dress a little more casually or flamboyantly, but, again, it pays to look twice and observe behavior as well. I astounded Katie Couric by guessing her birth order on the *Today Show*. She's a baby, but, of course,

she dresses like a first born for national television. But even though Katie Couric was groomed to the teeth, her fun, sparkling, engaging manner gave her away. She was just plain enjoying what she did—a classic sign of a baby of the family.

2. Personality wise, your typical babies of the family are friendly, easygoing, and playful. They exhibit a sense of humor and seem confident and secure. Last borns are engaging from the very start. You get the feeling you've known them for years after just two minutes of conversation. That was certainly the case with Katie Couric.

> *E*ven though Katie Couric was groomed to the teeth, her fun, sparkling, engaging manner gave her away. She was just plain enjoying what she did—a classic sign of a baby of the family.

3. As for mannerisms and speech, last borns are flamboyant, humorous, bold, assertive, and often verbose. Last borns are less inclined to be detail oriented—they like the flash, glitter, etc.

4. Last borns' offices could very well look like they are well lived in—even a tad messy. Their knickknacks might include little figures, stuffed animals, or toys that all suggest a desire to relax and have fun.

On the wall in my office is a large blowup of a cartoon from a feature article on my counseling techniques that appeared in a local newspaper. It shows an arrow with a suction cup stuck to my forehead as I'm looking down in surprise at a defiant little boy who has obviously just fired on me. Also hung on the walls are blown-up newspaper articles that discuss birth order and what it has to do with human behavior.

I don't put all this stuff on the wall to make my office into a "birth order shrine." I do it to give people a little bit of a feel for who I am and what I have to say. And, of course, I also hope to entertain them a bit while they are paying a visit to see "Dr. Leman, the psychologist."

5. Last borns do not reflect much compulsive behavior, but they can be "all over the place," handling several things at once. If you get the feeling you're in organized chaos, you are probably dealing with a last born.

What If Someone Doesn't "Fit" the Right Birth Order?

Now is as good a time as any to tell you that you're bound to have it happen: Someone displaying first-born characteristics such as neatness, being well groomed, meticulous in speech, thought, and dress, will turn out to be a middle child or even a baby of the family! The basic or typical characteristics of each birth order are there, but they have been altered, and sometimes changed radically, by certain circumstances or forces.

There is always an explanation for these characteristics that don't seem to match, and that explanation always lies with a word that is important to understanding how birth order theory really works—*variables*. If I'm going to assess all your birth order *characteristics*, there are several questions I need to have answered. And the answers to these questions are the variables that will explain why you can run across people who are one birth order but act like another.

First, what is your sex? If you're Pat Williams, general manager of the Orlando Magic NBA basketball team that went to the finals in 1995, I learn that you're the only boy in the family with an older sister and two younger sisters. Does that make you a middle child? You will probably have middle-child characteristics, but you're also the *first-born boy* in your family and that means that you are likely to take on some first-born traits, which Pat certainly did. He has been a manager of some kind all his life.

Or suppose you're Lee Iacocca, second born in a family of two with an older sister. Again, while you were born last, you're the *first-born boy* in the family. When I mix in the values of your Italian parents (more on that in a moment), I find an only son who has pushed hard to succeed from Day One.

Although not all of my Adlerian colleagues would agree, my general rule of thumb is that if you're the first of your sex born in the family, you are almost sure to have some first-born characteristics.

Second, what is the spacing? That is, how many years are there between you and the siblings immediately above and below you? A rule of thumb held by most psychologists who use birth order is that any time there is at least a five-year gap between children, a "new family" starts, so to speak.

For example, when I interviewed Herb Kelleher, president and CEO of Southwest Airlines, regarding this book, I mentioned that I first read about him in a business column where he had been quoted concerning how he and his staff had built Southwest Airlines into one of the most profitable operations anywhere. He said: "We defined a personality as well as a market niche. [We seek to] amuse, surprise, and entertain."[2]

I had written next to that quote, "Herbie must be a baby." When I interviewed him, however, I learned that, while he was indeed the baby of the family (fourth born of four) there was a very large gap between him and his next oldest brother—nine years. Any time you have that big a gap between siblings, what has basically happened is a new family of birth order has started over again.

In Herb Kelleher's case, he was last born with siblings who

were nine, thirteen, and fourteen years older than he. With all these siblings who were so much bigger, stronger, and more capable than he, Herb grew up much like a first born who had five "parents." With all that coaching and all those capable people to model after, it's no wonder Herb made it to the top and became the CEO of a prominent airline.

And that's why Herb is a mixed bag. He's fun to talk to—probably more fun than any other CEO or president of a company I've ever met. But at the same time, he does have that baby side and he loves to enjoy himself. Lately, Southwest is running TV commercials in our area that cast Kelleher as a referee who calls unnecessary roughness penalties on luggage handlers who are too tough on the merchandise. It's obvious Herb wants to make life fun, to entertain, and to amuse.

If you've ever been on a Southwest Airlines flight, you have probably experienced exactly what Herb has been talking about. I flew on Southwest recently, and the flight attendant opened her spiel by singing a song to the tune of "Oscar Mayer Wiener." "My airline has a first name, it's S-O-U-T-H. . . . My airline has a second name, it's W-E-S-T." And she went on from there to soon put us all in stitches.

When I mentioned this to Kelleher, he said, "That's not part of our training program. We don't force attendants to be entertainers. We just tell them if they feel comfortable doing things like that, great! And if they feel uncomfortable, don't bother. They actually come up with many of these things themselves."

Third, what are the differences between you and the siblings immediately above or below you? Suppose, for example, a first-born girl is small and of average intelligence, but her sister, born three years later, is attractive, tall, an excellent athlete, and a good student to boot. What can easily happen here is what we call a *role reversal*, with the second-born child actually taking over the first born's mantle of leadership, accomplishment, and privilege.

While this didn't happen totally to Thomas Watson, Jr., who became president of IBM, there were plenty of role reversal overtones in regard to his brother, Dick, five years his junior. In his biography, Watson admits that in many ways Dick was his superior—better grades, better athlete, with a natural command of languages. Dick had an easy way of relating to people that made him appear much more gracious, relaxed, and charming than his older brother. While Thomas, Jr., had to serve a long and hard apprenticeship of six years to gain a substantial position in his father's business, Dick was put in charge of all of IBM's foreign operations after only eight months as a salesman. Tom, Jr., bitterly protested and this caused considerable friction and jealousy for years.[3]

Fourth, what are the birth orders of your parents? This is a key question because it speaks about parenting style. Typically, a parent will overidentify with a child of his or her own birth order. For example, suppose you have two first-born parents who have two sons. You can almost bet that Mom and Dad are perfectionists and the pressure on the older boy will be fierce.

On the other hand, suppose the parents are a middle-child wife and a last-born husband, and they have three daughters. The first born would get some pressure, because first borns always do. But that last born will really get away with murder as she's doted on by her last-born dad.

Fifth, what were your parents' values? When assessing birth order traits, this is often the most pervasive variable of all. Sometimes parental values can override almost everything else. For a good example of what I'm talking about, let's take a quick look at Lee Iacocca of Ford and Chrysler fame.

Guess Who Made Lee Run?

Reading Lee Iacocca's biography quickly reveals how parental values can mold a powerful business figure. Lee's sister, Delma, was born first. Then a couple of years later he came along to become the first-born son in the family. When you become acquainted with Iacocca's parents, you also see the variable of family values coming into play in a big way. They were Italian immigrants who loved their children dearly but were always pushing them to "be the best you can be."

Iacocca was an interesting blend of a second-born "baby of the family" and the first-born boy who got all kinds of pressure and prodding to perform, particularly from his father. When Iacocca graduated twelfth in a class of over nine hundred in his high school, his father complained: "Why weren't you *first*?"

"To hear him describe it," writes Iacocca, "you'd think I flunked!"[4]

Fortunately, Iacocca's parents tempered their enthusiasm and encouragement with plenty of love. Iacocca and his father were very close. He writes:

> I loved pleasing him, and he was always terrifically proud of my accomplishments. If I won a spelling contest at school, he was on top of the world. Later in life whenever I got a promotion, I'd call my father right away and he'd rush right out to tell all his friends. . . . In 1970, when I was named president of the Ford Motor Company, I don't know which of us was more excited.[5]

It's no exaggeration to say that Iacocca's family had everything to do with his becoming a man of incredible resilience and steely resolve. After being fired by Ford he masterminded a comeback from the dead by Chrysler. His style—aggressive, decisive, straightforward, passionate, volatile, funny, someone who tells it like it is—can be traced right back to how that first-born son grew up in a loving Italian home in Allentown, Pennsylvania.

Lee Iacocca is a prime example of why you should *never discount the power of your family*. The influence of your family will reach across a town, a state, a country, to touch you in profound and sometimes disturbing ways years after you think you have grown up and "gotten beyond all that." Who you are because of your birth order has a great deal to do with how effective you are in your profession or place of employment. Birth order heavily influences how well or how poorly you get along with others. As I will explain in Chapter Seven, it could well be that there are certain birth orders you should not work for or work with, if you can possibly help it.

Small Talk Can Pay Big Dividends

I've said it before, but I'll say it again for emphasis: *It's never a good idea to ask direct questions about somebody's birth order.* For example, do not say something like: "You're always so well dressed and nicely groomed, tell me, are you the first born in your family, or at least the first-born male [or female]?"

This kind of question will make you sound like one of two things: a first-year psychology student doing research for a term paper, or a mental case.

A much better approach is to engage the other person in conversation and ask casual questions such as, "Where did you grow up? Where's home for you?"

As you get the customer talking about where he grew up, you have him talking about his family. From there you can ask what his family did—were they farmers? Was there a family business? Did he have any brothers or sisters? Was it a large or small family?

The other person might respond: "It was just me and my sisters and my kid brother."

To this you could comment, "I'll bet the kid brother got away with murder."

More than likely the other person will say, "Yeah, he did, as a matter of fact."

"So you had to do most of the work?" you could say. "Tell me, who was oldest in the family—you or your sisters?"

With this kind of an approach, you always want to be casual, with your goal to form a relationship first and get birth order specifics later. Keep making mental notes as you build a case for whatever birth order this person might be.

Another approach is to bring up something about your own family rather casually. For example, "I saw my older brother over the weekend. He and his family came down for the holidays. Do you have any siblings who descend on you at holiday time?"

As you engage in discovering a person's birth order, you are learning all kinds of things: hobbies, favorite sports, favorite teams, favorite restaurants, the possibilities are almost endless. If your first conversation is in the customer's office, you might spot a golf trophy on the shelf and casually observe—"I see you picked up a golf trophy or two. You must play pretty well."

"I play a bit," your new friend may respond. From there you can get his handicap, where he plays, and even invite him along to fill out your foursome.

For Perfectionists, Golf Can Be Life or Death

Once on a golf course or in any number of other athletic settings, there are all kinds of things you can learn about people and their approach to life. I recall playing in Tucson on a little par-three course with my friend Bill Foster, who, like me, was born last in his family. We both play golf for laughs, and when we go out together we just plain have a good time, no matter where our tee shots wind up or how many putts we take.

We were on the third tee headed one way, and across a small canyon another pair of golfers were heading in the other direction off the seventh tee across a lake. Suddenly, we heard someone turning the air blue with a barrage of expletives and we looked up in time to see a man, who had obviously dubbed his tee shot into the lake, proceed to throw his club into the water. This should have been enough to vent his frustration, but apparently he had been having a *very* bad round. He then picked up his *entire golf bag* and threw it into the drink! As the man stormed off with his playing partner, now sans any clubs, I looked at Bill and said with a wink, "I love golf, don't you? It's such a relaxing game."

It wasn't too hard to take an educated guess on the birth order of the guy who had just deep-sixed all his gear. He was probably an only child, at least a first born, and a perfectionist for whom golf was not a game but life or death.

The more personal knowledge you can gain of a customer (or someone you hope to make a customer) the better because it will all help give you some clues about that person's "private logic." We all have our own unique and individual private logic—a very personal overview of how we see life, how we see others, and how we see ourselves.

Our private logic is more or less our personal agenda. Each of us views life differently. If you doubt this, call two or three of your siblings or close friends with whom you have shared a memorable experience in the past. Simply ask: "Do you remember the time . . . ?" Describe the experience in a few words, then sit back and listen as you hear amazingly different views on what happened.

Always be aware of your customer's private logic. As you try to understand his or her point of view, it is here that you really "get behind your customer's eyes." It is here you learn about the person's real biases, preferences, and desires. Mark it down:

LEMAN'S LAW #8:

All of us have a private logic—our own unique and biased view of life from behind our own eyes.

As you call upon your clients, keep making mental (and later written) notes about their birth order characteristics. Soon you will have an invaluable little "file" right on the back of a Rolodex card that will remind you of how they think, what they like, and how they want to do business. This information can become a literal gold mine, but, of course, the bottom line is how you mine that gold—that is, how you use this information in actual sales situations. We'll look at that in the next chapter as we consider the best way to sell to each of the three basic birth orders.

The Bottom Line

1. How interested am I in "getting behind the customer's eyes"? How can I improve in this area?

2. On a scale of one (nonexistent) to ten (excellent), how are my "personal info notes" on each of my customers?

3. What birth order are most of my customers? How can I use this chapter to sell and service them better?

CHAPTER FIVE

Using Birth Order Secrets to Make the Sale Every Time*

*well, almost

I have used the following "secrets" for years as I've dealt with the three basic birth orders: first borns, middle children, and last-born babies. Whether I'm selling myself as a speaker or counseling a client about how he might change if he chooses to do so, I use these tips almost automatically and instinctively.

In fact, I'm not the only one who sees the value in using knowledge of personality traits to succeed in business. So does my friend and colleague Bill Johnson, who is president of his own management and consulting company in Phoenix. He also conducts management seminars and has served as executive vice-president of the National Speakers Association, which is where I met him several years ago. I receive material from Bill from time to time, and as I read a short one-page article he had written, "Managing and Selling Different People Differently,"[1] a light began to dawn.

As I went over tips on "Dealing with Dan and Danielle Direct," and learned that "Orderly Is Your Clue with Ollie and Olivia Organized," I realized, "Why, he's describing first borns and only children to a 'T'!" And when I read the paragraph on "Selecting Behavior with Sue and Sam Steady," it was clear that he was talking about middle children.

The final paragraph of Bill's article suggested, "Actions with Ann and Andy Animated," and that clinched it. Bill had me—a last-born baby—cold. Although he had never used the words *birth order* in his article, he had done a great job of describing classic birth order traits, and the idea for the book you are reading was born. So what follows aren't really "secrets." They are simple, commonsense concepts that you can use when selling to any of the major birth orders.

Secrets to Selling to First Borns

Selling to a first born (or the only child who is a super first born) is a little like clearing a mine field. You need to proceed with caution, but you want to get in and out as quickly as possible.

If you asked a first-born purchasing agent to tell sales reps how to turn him off, those sales reps would undoubtedly hear the following:

1. Give me the impression you think you know it all.

2. Be pushy.

3. Don't be well organized or concerned about having enough facts.

Keep in mind that when talking to a first born, you're talking to Mr. Nuts and Bolts, Mr. Specifications Page. He is not likely to be overly impressed with flashy four-color brochures and lots of bold claims. The first born basically wants to know: "What is your product or service going to do for me?" and "How much will it cost?" So proceed with caution with first borns and watch out for red lights.

Getting in the Door and off the Ground

First, it never hurts to do all you can to clear the yellow brick road to the Wizard of Oz. In other words, it's a good idea to call ahead and talk to the secretary (who is probably also a first born). Ideally, you know her first name already because you learned it when you called the first time to set up an appointment. This time you say: "Rose, I'm just calling to confirm my appointment with Mr. Hennesey for three o'clock this afternoon. I'm planning to be there a few minutes early because I know how busy he is and I don't want to waste one minute of his time waiting for me."

*I*f you want to turn off a first-born purchasing agent: Give the impression you know it all. Be pushy. Don't be well organized or concerned about having enough facts.

This kind of call accomplishes several things: 1. You confirm your appointment—that Mr. Hennesey will still be available at the agreed upon hour; 2. You create the impression that you're efficient and well organized; 3. You acknowledge the secretary as a person as you call her by her name and chat with her. This gives you a start on making her your ally but it's possible there is even more that you can do once you arrive in the office.

Suppose, for example, you arrive and you're waiting for a few moments in the reception area as Rose works at her desk nearby. You note a grandchild's picture and you comment, "What a beautiful little girl—is she your grandchild?"

If Rose says, "Why, yes, she is," you have struck gold. Just sit back and ask, "Tell me about your granddaughter."

As Rose waxes eloquent about her granddaughter, be sure to remember the baby's name and age. These are vital notes for your Rolodex or notebook file. And the next time you call, of course, you will ask, "How's little Emily?"

But now the moment's come to be ushered into Mr. Hennesey's office. To grab his first-born attention switch, you must be prepared. Remember that Mr. Hennesey is a very direct, no-nonsense, bottom-line kind of guy. If you don't get right to the point, he might just point you to the door.

So you have your sales pitch planned and you follow it to the letter. You don't ramble, you don't try to fake it, you say your piece, preferably in five minutes, three would be even better.

Why First Borns Hate the Question *Why*?

As you give your presentation to a first born, you may hear him asking questions like "Why?" along with "What?" "When?" "Where?" and "How much?" Be ready to answer all those questions, of course, but whatever you do, try not to ask the first born any questions beginning with "Why." Naturally, you're probably wondering, *Why not?* Because the question "Why?" is confrontive and puts the other person on the defensive, at least a little bit, but sometimes more than a little bit.

*W*hatever you do, try not to ask the first born any questions beginning with "Why?"

For the first born, especially, a question beginning with "Why" is a threat to his or her being in control. Always remember that first borns like to be in control, and they are not at all pleased by surprises or questions that might put them on the defensive.

It's also good not to press the first born for a decision. I'm not saying you shouldn't try to close a sale; we'll get to that in a moment. But remember that first borns like plenty of detail, so encourage feedback as you proceed.

And don't be overly concerned when the first born lacks enthusiasm as you hand him your beautiful brochures. He likes handouts, but he usually wants bottom-line facts, numbers, and specifications.

One other thing to remember is that first borns have substantial egos. When you have an opening you might want to ask the first born what makes him or his company successful. Be cautious, however, about saying anything that sounds like insincere flattery. In fact, if you really want to impress Mr. Hennesey, try to do some homework on his company before you arrive. If the company is listed on the stock exchange, you can call a broker and try to get updated on the latest action regarding that firm.

Another excellent resource for doing homework on a potential client is your public library. Back issues of magazines and local newspapers may give you all kinds of background on this company's past problems, its plans, and needs for the future.

Nobody is a bigger advocate of doing your homework than Harvey Mackay. In *Swim With the Sharks Without Being Eaten Alive*, he describes the "Mackay 66"—a 66-question customer profile kept on everyone that Mackay Envelope Corporation deals with. The Mackay 66 is invaluable for keeping everyone up to speed on the company's top accounts. For the first ten years the "66" was in use, Harvey would take home the files on his ten top accounts over weekends and drill the information into his head until he knew it by rote.[2]

Closing the Sale with a First Born

As you wrap up your presentation, always keep in mind that first borns want to know the cons as well as the pros, the negatives as well as the positives. Don't try to fool them by claiming what you are selling is absolutely foolproof and flawless. You know better and so do they.

Instead, use the psychological principle of "oppositional attraction." It's the same thing that I've often used with small children in counseling situations. Way back in graduate school, we learned that if you move *toward* the average two-year-old, saying, "Come here, come to me," he will usually go the other way—as fast as his little feet will carry him. But if you want to get the average two-year-old to come to you, you *back up* and say, "Come, come to me." When I first heard this I didn't believe it would work, but in nine cases out of ten it actually does. There is something about backing up that leaves the child feeling in control and not as fearful.

And what does handling two-year-olds have to do with handling forty-five-year-old purchasing agents or CEOs? A great deal. The idea is that you don't just make your sales pitch saying, "Please sign with me and my company." Instead, as you move toward your close, you will want to let the first born know he is in control—he's the one who will make the decision. One of the best ways to do this is to state the obvious pluses and minuses. For example:

> "Now I know that you have been with this other company for seven or eight years and they've been giving you good service. I'd be lying if I said only we give good service—lots of companies give good service. But what I'm excited about is the new dimensions of what we offer. We are ahead of our competitors in several areas. We've not only broken ground, we've established ourselves and we have a proven product [or service]."

. . . or

> "Because you're a key industry in this town, I'm prepared to give you a program that will be difficult for you to turn down, yet I realize you may turn it down. Seven years of good experience with another firm is hard to overcome. I know that. We can probably beat them by a quarter of a million a year, but they have that good track record and you may elect to stay with them because of that record. I respect that, but I just ask you to consider what we're offering, because I know we can do a bang-up job for you."

Then leave it with the first born. You've made your pitch and he will make his own decision. If things have gone well, you may hear him say something like: "I want to think this over. I know someone [across town, in the next state, etc.] who uses your product [or service]. I think I'll give them a call and see what they think."

On the other hand, you may hear a polite, "Thank you very much. I appreciate your presentation and we'll be letting you know."

In many cases, especially with first borns, the latter comment is probably what you will get when making a first call. All you're really trying to do on this first call is get your toe in the door. Your foot can come later.

To Sum Up Selling to a First Born

1. Be on time, be prepared, and get right to the point.

2. Be ready for plenty of questions, but never ask the first born, "Why?"

3. Have plenty of facts, specs, and numbers at your fingertips. Don't rush, instead move at a brisk pace through your very organized presentation.

4. Stroke the first born's ego but don't use any kind of insincere flattery. Ask him about his company and its accomplishments to help break the ice.

5. Use oppositional attraction as you close the sale. That is, be honest about any negative points and, if possible, have options he can choose from.

6. Once finished, let the first born make his decision. Don't be pushy. Always make it clear that he is in control.

As a group, first borns are formidable but reachable. They're impressed by efficiency and a concern for their time and busy schedule. With first borns, remember:

LEMAN'S LAW #9:

Don't try to get chummy, just get done and get out.

Secrets to Selling to the Middle Child

We've been saying it throughout this book, but we'll stop right here to say it again: *Sales are relational.*

Probably no other birth order is more sensitive to this axiom than the middle child. Middle children are relational by nature because they have a hunger for it. As you will remember, they are the ones who went outside the family first to find friends and groups where they felt somewhat in control and not squeezed as they did at home.

*T*he middle child actually enjoys being asked questions—in fact, the more questions the better.

As you prepare to call on a middle child, you want to remember that he is a good team player, reliable, steady, and loyal. And, unlike the first born, he actually enjoys being asked questions—in fact, the more questions the better. Why is this? It's simple: He never got asked that many questions while growing up at home. He was simply ignored.

While most middle children tend to be more laid back and relational, there are exceptions. You can run into a middle child who is something of a buzz saw—very competitive, even a scrappy aggressor type. And instead of seeming to like relationships, the middle child might be a loner, quiet, or shy. It has been my observation, however, over years of counseling, that the typical middle child who winds up in some kind of middle management position, where he is making decisions regarding purchasing supplies or services, is more inclined to be the relational negotiator and mediator.

Some Ideas on Approaching the Middle Child

When calling on relationship-hungry middle children, you may want to ask them if there is anybody else they would like to bring along—to sit in on the conversation or to go to lunch perhaps. With a third party, it's often easier to keep conversation flowing and this may put the middle child at ease. But it is the middle child's call and not yours. Never bring along one of your own colleagues as a "surprise," thinking that the relationship-hungry middle child believes "the more the merrier." Middle children like relationships, but on their terms. Otherwise you could easily wind up making the middle child feel overwhelmed.

Another good idea is to contact the middle child outside the office—at lunch, for example. Do everything you can to make your call less the sales call and more the social contact. The middle child usually responds best to a slower presentation, given with sensitivity. If it's a first call, you may want to leave the impression that you're not there to sell something as much as you are just to make a contact and get to know each other.

Do everything you can to convince the middle child you are concerned about him and his particular interests. If he is a small businessman and your company usually sells to bigger firms, let him know that that doesn't make him any less important to you. For example, you might be able to say: "We've just opened a new division to accommodate small businesses, and I'd like to show you a package that will save you money."

Another effective approach to the middle child is to ask him what his biggest problem or hurdle is. What's the greatest difficulty he faces in business today? Learn how you can help with this and then move in to do just that. For example: "I'd like to invite you down to our plant. I'd like you to see what we can do for you."

A variation of this could be: "I'd like to invite you down to meet some of our people. I want to show you what we're doing for businesses like yours on a regular basis."

You'll probably have to make more calls on a middle child before you close the sale. Build your relationship slowly, cast out your lines, and wait. As a rule, middle children may need more lines cast than the decisive first borns or the more impetuous babies. The middle child is more go-with-the-flow. He may take longer to sell, but in the end he may be a more loyal customer (if you give him good service).

Middle Children Like the Warm Fuzzies

Again, remember middle children are more likely to appreciate the old proven ways. Their motto is definitely, "If it ain't broke, why fix it?" or, "If I've been getting along fine with the product from XYZ Company, why should I switch to ABC Company?" Obviously, price can be a factor, but it isn't always the main consideration. Middle children, in particular, will be looking for service, for relationships, for the warm fuzzy kind of thing that will help them feel more secure and more at home with you as a supplier.

Middle children are not as afraid of (or as disturbed by) change as first borns might be. First borns like the status quo because it helps them stay in control. But because the middle child never had that much control while growing up, he's a little more willing to roll with the punches.

And while middle children may not be as perfectionistic as first borns, that doesn't mean that you can't find a middle child who isn't a perfectionist. Any birth order can succumb to perfectionism. It's just that first borns and only children are more likely to do so because of the tremendous pressure they have been under ever since they can remember.

Coming back to the idea of casting lines and reeling in the middle child slowly, remember that he does not like confrontation of any kind. In other words, take your time, never push, and always use the softer sell. The typical middle child might respond well to your calling up and suggesting that you drop by with a little take-out food. Then you can add: "We can sit down right there at the desk, roll up our sleeves, and look at some numbers."

Obviously, if you make this kind of invitation to the middle child, you already know that he or she isn't big on going out to lunch. You've done some prior probing and you know that this person is more than happy to work through lunch at the desk and often does so anyway.

My insurance agent and I "work through lunch" quite often. I'm more than happy to sit down with him over a sandwich and talk business. In this regard, I'm much like a middle child. I appreciate the closer intimacy of just getting together in the office over a sandwich.

As You Close the Sale with a Middle Child

And while the money-back guarantee or no-obligation promises are always powerful tools with any birth order, they are particularly attractive to the middle child. Keep in mind that he is slightly insecure and still rebelling (maybe more than a little bit) against the childhood that had him in the middle, squeezed, left out, and sometimes ignored.

It never hurts to emphasize to middles how they can check with others about your claims and how you will specifically service them if they do buy anything from you. For example, you might say: "We both know there are many companies that do what we do. But I believe that the company I'm representing really focuses on fitting our product [or service] to a customer's needs. We will bend over backward to accommodate specifically what will enhance your production."

To Sum Up Selling to the Middle Child

1. Middle children hunger for relationships.

2. Middle children tend to be good team players, reliable, steady, and loyal. They are usually very concerned about how their decisions may affect others.

3. Middle children don't mind being asked questions. For some, the more questions you ask the better, especially if you show interest in them. Learn all you can about the middle child's family and background.

4. When you are making a contact with a middle child, invite him or her to have an assistant or colleague along, if that seems practical.

5. Middles like a slower, more sensitive presentation.

6. With the middle child, cast your line and wait.

7. Middle children like the old proven ways. Don't try to fix things for them right away.

8. Middle children like a softer, more sociable sell. If it's appropriate, bring along a small but nice personal gift for the middle child. Sometimes companies provide these items but, even if your company doesn't, spend a few dollars on something you know the middle child would like, particularly something with his or her name on it.

9. Middle children especially like personal service and your concern for *them*.

10. Middle children, in particular, like to receive a short note of congratulations or recognition.

When dealing with middle children, you must always remember one thing. To say it still one more time, as emphatically as I can:

LEMAN'S LAW #10:

Sales are relational.
Sales are relational.
Sales are relational.

Secrets to Selling to the Last-Born Babies

There is one more birth order that is, in some ways, more relational than the middle child. I speak, of course, of the babies of the family. When selling to last borns, I always like to say, "Bring your dancin' shoes and a weather vane." In other words, be as fun and as charming as you can, and be aware that as the winds change the last born can change as well. Babies fly by the seat of their pants and they never stay put for very long.

Sell Them Before They Sell You!

As you prepare to approach your last-born client or potential customer, the more entertaining you can be the better. It doesn't mean that you come prancing in with party hat and horn. All I'm saying is, your typical baby of the family is looking for fun in life and, while he or she may appear quite businesslike on the surface, this fun-oriented attitude can be right there waiting to come out.

If you think a social environment is good for approaching a middle child, it's even better for the last born. Babies of the family like to work hard and play hard. Sometimes they like to do both at the same time.

*W*hen selling to last borns, "bring your dancin' shoes and a weather vane" . . . as the winds change the last born can change as well.

For example, when a publishing house wants to do business with me and they know I'm a fisherman, it's a natural for an acquisition editor to invite me and maybe a couple of other people from his company to go fishing. That's where we can all have fun and I can let my hair down about certain things that may be bothering me.

Or, perhaps you are just trying to get started with a prospect who is a last born and you need an introduction. This could be a perfect place to bring in a mutual friend and have everyone get together at lunch.

In certain situations it might be appropriate to invite spouses along for lunch or dinner. Remember, however, that if you bring your spouse and the last born brings his or her spouse, the contact has really turned into a social occasion and there will probably be very little opportunity to get business done. That's not to say the event couldn't be very valuable because it would build a relationship and lay groundwork for future negotiations.

As you're chatting with your last-born customer, be aware that he always loves hearing or telling a good story or joke. Ask, "Would you tell me some of your favorite stories—things that have happened in your business? I'd love to hear them."

When you tell stories, however, stay away from anything even remotely off-color. As much as I love humor, I always follow this rule, not because I think it's a safer way to do business, but because it's the best way to do business in any setting.

Time Counts, So Keep Things Moving

As you'll recall, we mentioned that you need to move fast with first borns because they are all business and have no time to waste. Last borns may want to waste a bit of time, but balanced against that is their short attention span. In fact, if your last-born client starts having fun with a story or two, you better be well aware of the time. It may be up sooner than you would have liked and your baby might be gone or halfway out the door, headed for another engagement or appointment, before you've had an opportunity to sell your product.

As you make your presentation, be aware that the typical baby of the family is highly susceptible to being impressed by name-dropping. It won't hurt at all to mention highly visible people or firms who already use your product or service.

Closing the Sale with a Last Born

The typical last born is 180 degrees from the typical first born. You'll remember that first borns could care less about full-color photos and slick looking layouts. They want the specs, the numbers, the graphs. Babies, on the other hand, could care less about specs, numbers, and graphs. They love those full-color pictures, the flash, and the glitter. That's how babies arrive at the bottom line.

In other words, the baby tends to ask first, "What does this whole thing really do for *me*? Does it make *me* feel good?" I'm not saying the baby can't make sound business decisions; I am saying that when it comes to weighing the business side of things against personal pluses and minuses, the baby will be giving the personal side significant weight.

Last Borns Are Often Risk Takers

At the same time, studies show that the later borns in the family, particularly babies, are far more likely to be risk takers than first borns. A professor of marketing from a major university in the South called me on one occasion to say she had just read *The Birth Order Book* and loved it. She speculated that because first borns are such leaders and the ones who move things forward in so many areas in life, it would make sense to know what first borns were thinking in order to predict the next trends in marketing.

The baby tends to ask first, "What does this whole thing really do for me? Does it make me feel good?"

I was impressed with how she was trying to use what she had been learning in *The Birth Order Book*, but I had to say, "You're absolutely right, first borns are the leaders of society, the evidence is overwhelming, but if you are looking for trends, you want to see what the later borns are doing. They're the ones who are far more likely to be willing to take a risk and to change things."

I continue to see reports on birth order studies that confirm that first borns want to support the status quo while later borns are far more likely to institute change. One of the most interesting studies I have run across is that of Frank Sulloway, a historian who has written an eight-hundred-page thesis with more than three hundred thousand entries on six thousand people involved in thirty scientific and social revolutions over the past five hundred years.

Sulloway discovered that later borns will often pounce on new ideas. For example, in the 1830s they went for phrenology, the theory that says bumps on the skull reveal your personality. Later borns also tend to be revolutionaries. For example, many of the leaders of the Protestant Reformation were later borns.[3]

Knowing that last borns tend to be risk takers can help you as you move in to close your presentation. Because they want to act now, not later, babies are typically spontaneous and impetuous. You can be a little more confrontative and press a little harder for a decision. If the baby of the family is leaning at all in your direction, don't hesitate to ask for a commitment or to sign on the bottom line.

When I bought that Chrysler Sebring convertible recently, I went in and made the deal I wanted to make, true enough, but the sales manager—a first born, by the way, who was a very dapper dresser—also did a good job of recognizing how I was operating and he dealt with me accordingly. For example, he noticed I was in a hurry and impatient. Maybe he even remembered that I tend to be a bit impetuous because he had dealt with me before. At any rate, he didn't hem and haw. He made the deal, signed me up, and let me drive out the door in a very short time. In other words, while he'd never had any kind of course on selling to different birth orders, he sold me—a last born—pretty well.

To Sum Up Selling to a Baby of the Family

1. Be ready to mix a little fun and charm with being businesslike.

2. Have your emotional wind gauge along—babies fly by the seat of their pants, so keep your eyes open.

3. For a first contact, a social setting is always good.

4. Have a couple of good stories or jokes ready, but nothing off-color.

5. Keep your presentation moving—the baby's attention span is short.

6. If possible, drop names or other information that will impress the impressionable baby.

7. Warm fuzzies and a little flash and glitter will be at least as important as specs and hard info.

8. Remember babies are impetuous, so don't be afraid to press for a decision.

9. Never let an attempt to be light, fun, or social look like a lack of respect for the last born.

Selling to babies can be fun, but don't get the idea they're airheads. Remember that there is that dark side to the baby—the side that says, "I want to *show them*!" Last borns remind us of a universal truth:

LEMAN'S LAW #11:

**All of us want respect,
some of us more than others.**

The Bottom Line

1. What do I need to remember most when selling to the first borns who are among my clients? Who in particular comes to mind right now?

2. What do I need to remember most about clients who are middle children? What can I try in order to be more relational?

3. Do I have any babies of the family among my clients? Am I being careful to give last-born clients plenty of respect?

A Pop Quiz on Birth Order

Following are typical statements certain birth orders would make while being called on. See if you can identify who is talking—a first born, a middle child, or a last born. (Put F, M, or L next to each statement.)

1. ___ "Tell me again, who was it you said used your product?"

2. ___ "So what can I do for you? I don't have a lot of time, so I hope this won't take too long."

3. ___ "Just a minute, I'd like to get my assistant in here to take a look at this, too."

4. ___ "Tell me again, how many colors does this come in? I hope you've got something that's bright and alive."

5. ___ "Okay, okay, slow down and give me the specs in one-two-three order."

6. ___ "Well, if you can't sell them by the gross, how about by the dozen? I'm sure you're willing to work this out."

7. ___ "Look, I'm due on the first tee in twenty minutes. Let's have the bottom line. What is this really going to do for me and my company?"

8. ___ "I just don't know. . . . We've used the XYZ Corporation's widget for almost fifteen years. They have a good track record."

9. ___ "I think I have the picture. I'll be letting you know."

10. ___ "That's very nice, but I'm not much for graphs or statistics. What's it gonna cost me?"

Answers:
1. L; 2. F; 3. M; 4. L; 5. F; 6. M; 7. F; 8. M; 9. F; 10. L.

CHAPTER SIX

Relationships—Sales Are All about Relationships

I was somewhere in an airport as usual, waiting for the next plane, when I decided to kill some time wisely by whipping out my little tape player and earphones and listening to Tom Peters, author of *Thriving on Chaos* and other best-sellers on the changing business scene. Peters always makes good sense but as I sat there enjoying his tape and making notes, one particular comment hit me right between my last-born ears:

> Only companies that stay attached to their customers will survive and prosper.[1]

As I replayed that bit of tape several times, the same word kept coming to my mind—*relationships*. In fact, Tom Peters's admonition to "stay attached to your customers" became the basis for this chapter. As a baby of my family, I had been cuing in on relationships all my life. No one really ever had to tell me that the sales person who is continually successful is the one who builds strong relationships with customers. I sort of knew it intuitively, almost from the cradle.

Born third and last with a powerful athletic big brother and a super-capable big sister above me, it didn't take me long to decide that I couldn't compete with those two super stars who were so much bigger, stronger, faster, and smarter. So I took another route, always trying to make people laugh, always getting into something in order to get attention.

I decided academics was not my cup of tea. As I went through school, I squeaked by, barely passing, sometimes failing, and always playing the class clown who drove the teachers crazy.

As for sports, I was too small for football and too short for basketball. As a high school sophomore I thought I'd made the JV basketball team, but when the names went up on the board, mine was not among them and it almost killed me.

So I decided to settle on being a baseball player, which meant I usually saw action only during the first six weeks of the spring semester—before the grades came out. But every year I was out there, as long as they would let me, braving the unpredictable spring weather of western New York State. In those days, we used wooden bats, and you haven't lived if you've never felt the electrical shock reaching from the tips of your fingers all the way to the tips of your toes after you catch a half-frozen ball on the end of a Louisville Slugger.

I Started out by Selling Dirt

While life had its limitations, I never let them hold me back. From early on, I got attention and strokes from being an entertainer and "natural-born salesman." My magazine selling triumphs as a college sophomore weren't the first signs of my sales skills. Actually, I began getting experience while still very young.

For example, at the age of eight I would go up and down the block selling bags of dirt to the neighbors at ten cents a bag. How did I find customers? My "dirt business" was based on several secrets of success:

- I had a product everyone needed, whether they were planting a flower garden or plugging gopher holes.

- I kept my overhead low. My delivery truck was a Radio Flyer wagon, complete with those high wooden sides. It never needed a lube, an oil change, or a filter.
- I gave people excellent service, bringing the dirt right to their back doors.
- Most important, my sales were based on my friendships with the moms and dads in my neighborhood—especially the moms.

I realize my dirt selling story doesn't prove much except perhaps two things: First, everybody has to start somewhere, but the real point I'm trying to make is this:

LEMAN'S LAW #12:

People love to buy *anything*, especially if they like the person who is selling it to them.

From selling dirt I moved up to peddling vegetables from my own little roadside stand made of two card tables set up by a grassy parking strip, close to our driveway. The produce I sold came out of my own garden, where I raised red raspberries, tomatoes, currants, lettuce, radishes, and all kinds of other vegetables. I ran my little fruit and vegetable business for a couple of years and actually made a few dollars from time to time. The people seemed to like stopping to buy from the friendly little kid whose wares were always fresh and reasonably priced.

There's no telling how far I would have gone in the produce industry, but everything ended abruptly one day when my dad, who ran a dry cleaning shop in town, backed his truck out of the driveway. As he turned onto the street, he cut the wheels too sharply, and ran onto the parking strip where my stand was located. He didn't see it in time to stop, and in a few seconds my produce business became splinters and salsa.

And Just How Do You Build Relationships?

That sales is built on relationships is not exactly original news, especially for anyone in the selling profession. We all know we're supposed to get close to our customers and build relationships, but the question is, Are we doing it?

According to an informal survey by the National Association of Purchasing Managers, sales people don't always come across as being really ready or willing to do the kind of work that results in a relationship that will pay off for everyone. One purchasing manager who was surveyed said, "Sales people need to make sure their account is getting all that it needs—in terms of product, timely service, and technical assistance." The kind of sales person who is likely to get a typical purchasing agent's approval is the one who is honest, dependable, thorough, and who makes follow-through more than just a vague promise.[2]

I believe the above words are as true for me as they are for you. In fact, I feel still another Leman's Law coming on:

LEMAN'S LAW #13:

You build relationships one conversation, one call, one contact at a time.

I'm Interested Because I'm Really Interested

Two more attributes that I have found invaluable in building relationships are empathy and personal interest. As an author, I'm often out on the road pushing my latest book. My publisher sends me on a "tour" of several cities where I appear on TV and radio and then drop in at the local bookstores to greet and get to know people. I usually enjoy these bookstore stops a great deal. On rare occasions, however, I experience an author's worst nightmare: having a great TV or radio interview and then going downtown to stop at a bookstore and not finding my book anywhere!

I was in a large midwestern city not too long ago, being escorted about by a very classy lady who not only knows books, but she knows people, especially the managers of the bookstores. As she took me over to meet the manager of one bookstore that is part of a well-known national chain, she told me about how this manager's daughter had been in an accident. The damage had been so severe it had taken a year for the little girl to recover.

I told my escort I appreciated that information, and a few minutes later, when she introduced me to the bookstore manager, I said, "I hear you're quite a woman. I've heard some good things about you. I know it's been a rough year for you."

Immediately the bookstore manager perked up and the conversation jumped several levels above the usual perfunctory introduction. The reason was simple: With a couple of comments I had gone into a relationship kind of mode and let the lady know that I knew how it had been for her.

And then I added, "You know, I have four daughters myself."

That was all we really needed. The manager and I talked about her daughter's injuries and how her recovery had been slow and frustrating.

Later—quite a bit later, in fact—we got around to talking about why I was supposed to really be there—because I was in town on a book tour. It was as if a light went on and the store manager said, "Oh, my, what shows were you on today? Say, I don't think we have your book in stock. I'll order some right away!" In a few minutes, she put a sizable order for my book in the computer.

Later, as my escort drove me to the airport, we talked about the conversation I had had with the manager and she mentioned how impressed she had been with the way I could build a relationship so quickly. I commented, "You know, if you call that lady two years from now and mention my name, she'll remember me. Why? Because I was interested in *her* and *her child*, not primarily in pushing my books."

> *I* build relationships because *I am truly interested in the people I deal with.* The benefits that come out of that are obvious.

And that's the point of this little story. Obviously, I could go around being interested in bookstore managers (and everyone else) only to manipulate them to get what I want—more book sales. I want more book sales as badly as any author, but I can honestly say that I build relationships because *I am truly interested in the people I deal with*. The benefits that come out of that are obvious and, to some extent, automatic.

As someone said, "What goes around, comes around." If you always try to treat people the way you'd like to be treated, your motives will be right, and what comes around will almost always be good.

I Saw Coach K Get Blindsided

Every now and then I run into a leader who seems to understand intuitively why the Golden Rule isn't golden for nothing. One such person is Mike Krzyzewski, coach of the Duke University Blue Devils basketball team, who directs one of the most outstanding sports programs in the nation.

To even the most casual basketball fan, the name Krzyzewski (which most sportswriters mercifully shorten to "Coach K") is a household name. Before that disastrous season of 1994-95, when Coach K had to step down from handling the team because of a serious back ailment, Duke had been to the Final Four of the

NCAA tournament seven times in nine years. Five of those times they went to the final game and twice they won the title.

If you don't think a big-time college coach doesn't have to be a good salesman, you don't understand the situation. For one thing, he has to sell his school to prospects all the time. In fact, the first time I met Coach K, we were both on a flight headed for Buffalo. He was on a recruiting trip to see a promising young player in Ontario, Canada. We didn't have much time to talk, but I do remember asking him, "You have all the pressures of a CEO as you run a big-time sports program. How do you keep your personal life together?"

"That's easy," he replied. "We have a very close family and a lot of love." Before we landed I autographed a copy of *The Birth Order Book* for Mike's wife, Mickie, and we went our separate ways.

About a year later, I was on another airliner headed somewhere to speak when I looked across the aisle and there sat Mike and Mickie Krzyzewski! I didn't say anything at first, preferring to just watch them for a few minutes as our American Airlines 757 flew on toward the Dallas/Ft. Worth airport. Mickie was doing a crossword puzzle and Mike was working out of his briefcase, busy with personal correspondence.

Mickie must be a first born, I mused, *but I'm not so sure about Mike. The neatly organized briefcase and the note writing say he's a first born, too, but he's the only one in first class wearing Nike warmups . . .*

Could Mike Krzyzewski be a last born like me? I was riding in first class, wearing shorts myself. Finally I called across the aisle, "Excuse me, Mickie, did Coach K ever give you the book I autographed for you last year?"

She looked around startled, and then apparently recognized

my face from the picture on the book flap. "The birth order guy! I loved that book!"

Coach K pulled off the little half-glasses he was wearing to do his note writing and smiled. "Oh, yeah, I remember you . . ."

As I chatted with them for a few minutes I learned that, indeed, Mickie is a first born, but Mike is the second born of two sons. That didn't surprise me. While he's a baby of the family and, therefore, very personable with people, Mike obviously picked up some first-born traits while branching off the big brother above him. Then they both went back to what they had been doing— Mickie to her crossword puzzle, Mike to writing notes. As for me, I got out my briefcase and started straightening it up so it would look a little bit more like Coach K's.

After we landed, we all wrestled our carry-ons out of the upper storage compartments and started through the airport, heading for our connecting flights. I was walking a few feet behind the Krzyzewskis when I noticed a college-age kid hurrying by, headed the other way. There was a moving sidewalk between us, but once he spotted Coach K, that didn't stop him. He literally leaped over the moving sidewalk and ran back to catch up to Mike, exclaiming, "Coach, Coach, can I get your autograph?"

You can always tell when a leader or a manager really values people. It won't be revealed when he or she is making a big speech to the faculty or a presentation to the board of directors. It will show in the little moments when that leader is "off camera," so to speak, when he can be himself and few will be the wiser.

Coach K had every right at that moment to tell the young guy that he just couldn't stop, he was headed for another gate, and his plane might leave on him. Instead, he stuffed his two carry-ons between his knees, balanced the kid's piece of paper on his briefcase, and signed. As he handed the paper back to the obviously starstruck, stringy-haired collegian, Coach Mike

Krzyzewski, a basketball legend in his own time, said at least twice, "Thanks—thanks for asking."

Signing that autograph when he didn't really have any time wasn't unusual for Coach K. I believe it was a trademark kind of move, and one more example of the class act he takes everywhere he goes. He treats others as he himself would like to be treated and there is no better way to build relationships than that.

The Limo Driver Who Had a Special Touch

In my travels I find people with that special relational touch in the most interesting places. For example, when I do book tours and talk shows, I'm often hooked up with limo drivers for several days while visiting radio and TV stations in various cities. I noticed that one certain driver I rode with in a large midwestern metropolis would give gum and candy and other little treats to the toll booth people at the airport and on the toll roads. I was amazed because all those toll takers seemed to know him by name. The guy drove me around for two days and I kept noticing how hard he worked to put a smile on the faces of the people who sat in those little four- by six-foot booths all day long taking tolls.

For example, he'd just stop and ask for directions when obviously he didn't need directions. Among the gifts he would bring them would be a birthday cake and, while I rode with him, he delivered at least two cakes to toll takers.

I kept thinking, *Wow, this guy really knows these people if he knows them well enough to know their birthdays.* Finally, I could contain myself no longer and said, "I notice how friendly you are to the toll booth people. You even bring them birthday cakes—that's really unusual."

"They're people just like me," he said, with a "no big deal" tone in his voice. "I get to drive around all day, talk to people, see things. They're cooped up in that booth—it's like jail. I'm only doing what I'd want someone to do for me if I were in their place."

I've ridden in limos all over the country, but I've never seen the likes of that limo driver. He understands the Golden Rule. He knows how to win the rat race without becoming a rat.

Up in the Morning, out on the Loading Dock

One other personal story illustrates the value of building relationships whenever possible. I often meet with drivers for large book distribution companies. What I try to do is talk to the people who actually take the books out of the boxes and put them on racks in the stores. I give them a twenty-minute talk regarding my book and try to make it as entertaining and as funny as possible. Something else I usually do is take along some extra copies of the book and autograph one for each driver.

To make these talks, it usually means getting out of bed and getting down to the distribution company's loading dock at the crack of dawn. I've given my talk to as many as sixty drivers who would soon be leaving to take books all over the state to rack them in various stores. My motive is simple. I want them to know me and my books, so when it comes to a choice of putting Leman at eye level or ankle high, my books may have a better chance of winding up where someone would actually see the book cover.

*Y*ou can't FAX a relationship. It's something you have to do up close and personal.

Is all this effort worth it? I suppose there are some drivers who don't do anything differently because I came down to talk to them. They probably placed my book on the shelf at ankle height anyway. That's okay; I can't win them all. But I do believe I win quite a few with my presentation and my genuine attempt to build a relationship, even in that short time. My guess is they *do* remember me, for no other reason than they're impressed because I've made the effort. And believe me, I don't have a lot of competition. So far, I haven't exactly run into traffic jams getting into book distribution loading docks and briefing rooms at the crack of dawn.

But that is the name of the game—*to make the effort to build relationships*. One of the best TV commercials I've seen in a while is a pitch by Northwest Airlines for its business class customers. As they urge people to fly hither and yon to do business face to face, they remind us: "You can't FAX a handshake—you can't FAX a look in somebody's eye."

Come to think of it, you can't FAX a relationship. It's something you have to do up close and personal.

Relationships—Key to Positioning

As you build relationships, remember that *you are always positioning yourself* and in selling, position is everything.

Buyers, purchasing agents, and just everyday customers are suspicious by nature. As a sales representative you are constantly working at positioning yourself in a place where you can make the sale right now or at least get the account in the future. Harvey Mackay never worked for Avis, but he's a big believer in being Number Two. As I talked with him about sales strategies, I mentioned his view on positioning, which he explains in *Swim With the Sharks Without Being Eaten Alive.*[3]

"Getting into Number Two position isn't all that bad," I commented. "In fact, it's a profound thought."

"I just gave that speech yesterday and people were commenting on that," Harvey responded. "I came up with the 'work hard to be Number Two' concept about three and a half decades ago by using the Law of Large Numbers, which is an insurance term."

"How does the Law of Large Numbers work?" I asked.

"There are 262 million Americans living today," said Harvey, "and the insurance industry can tell you within one-quarter of 1 percent every year in the United States how many people are going to die—what age, what color, what sex, what creed. I decided to adapt the Law of Large Numbers and turn it into our sales philosophy. We have three thousand accounts—that's a lot of numbers—and we can't be Number One everywhere. But as long as we fight hard and stay focused and stand in enough lines as Number Two, eventually we're going to move up to Number One because of the Law of Large Numbers."

"What makes you so sure that you'll move up to Number One?"

"If I'm calling on you and you're the buyer at General Motors and I can't get the business, I know one thing. There is a probability that you're going to get fired, terminated, switch jobs, promoted, whatever, and there's going to be a new buyer coming in. Now that new buyer might not be in love with good old Number One, but I'm Number Two sitting right there."

"So, bang, you can jump right in and get the account?"

"Exactly," said Harvey, warming to his subject. "Also what can happen is the sales person representing the supplier who is currently Number One can be fired, terminated, promoted, leave, whatever, and now a new sales person will come in to represent the company that's Number One. But suppose the chemistry isn't that good between the new sales person and the buyer. Bang! I've got a chance again."

"So you're saying that the Law of Large Numbers works best when either the buyer or the sales person servicing the buyer is replaced?"

"Not always. Suppose you're my competitor calling on General Electric. You've had their business for five years and I want it back again. There's always the chance you might falter—fall on your face and not perform. When that happens, I'm right there. Also, suppose my company gets a new product, a new invention, a new idea. I can't just tell the General Electric buyer about it. I have to have had some vibes, be at least Number Two to be able to walk in and convince G.E. they need me. The key to being Number Two is always be ready to move in when Number One fades for whatever reason."

By the time Harvey Mackay finished explaining how he uses the Law of Large Numbers, I was doubly convinced that being Number Two isn't all that bad. Number One may be on the bubble and you're next to move in to make a sale and gain a very nice account.

The Power of the Short Note

Whether you're Number One or Number Two with a buyer, or whether you're simply trying to drum up some new prospects, one of your most useful tools can be "the short note." I've used short notes for years myself, and I was pleasantly impressed to see that Harvey Mackay includes a brief mention of them in his own writings. He points out that he uses short notes profusely, and many of the successful people he knows do as well, including Lou Holtz, Notre Dame football coach; Pat Fallon, chairman of the country's hottest advertising agency; Wheelock Whitney, who built one of the nation's most successful brokerage firms.[4]

Short notes are excellent ways to follow up an initial contact with a prospect or to continue to build a relationship with a new customer. They are also great for sending congratulations to someone who has just passed a notable milestone or who has enjoyed an important achievement.

Recently, for example, I wrote to a young woman who had been named dean of students at the University of Arizona. She's someone I knew years ago when I worked at the University. At that time she was just a young kid working in the financial aid office. Now she was dean, and my note said:

> *It was so nice to see that the University decided to pick one of their own. Continued best wishes and success. We're proud of you.*

I love to write notes to people who hit a benchmark or become successful. It takes time, true, but it pays big dividends. In a spiritual sense, this is how any of us really grow—when we can be really happy for other people and see that they are part of the big picture.

Sometimes my short notes turn into brief letters, like the one I sent recently to a teacher who had been written up in our local Tucson paper after a long and productive career in our school system. I blush to admit I did not get this letter off the day I saw the article, but in this case I thought, *Better late than never:*

*T*here has to be more to selling than simply trying to make a buck.

> *I just want you to know how proud I was for you when I read the wonderful article enclosed. I'm sure those many tributes to you from your former students had to make you feel that your thirty-plus years of teaching were more than worth it. You're to be congratulated. I hope you have a great retirement. Enjoy life to the fullest. You deserve it.*
>
> *Again, congratulations on a tremendous career. You really made a difference in kids' lives. Thanks for being a part of our lives here in Tucson.*

I'm not suggesting that the above samples are just what you ought to write to your customers or other business contacts. They are, however, simple models of how to show your interest and goodwill. Your particular note may just be a basic, "It was great to get together yesterday. I was really happy to learn more about you and your company's needs. I hope we can do it again soon."

You have to determine what you want to put in your note and for what purpose. The point is, use notes or brief letters to solidify any contacts you make and to build relationships with customers or colleagues. The business buzzword is *networking*, and no sales person can build too big a network because you never know where that next lead or sale may come from.

Looking at short notes from a birth order point of view, the most receptive people will be middle children. The typical middle child—who puts such an emphasis on relationships and friendships—will really be impressed by a personal note or brief letter. That's not to say that last borns or first borns should not receive notes or letters. It is to say that with middle children, in particular, this can be a *very* effective sales tool. Short notes build relationships, which will lead to business in the long run.

But along with all the sales and new accounts you hope to gain, there is one benefit that is possibly even more important: building relationships with other people and, in some cases, even friendships. There has to be more to selling than simply trying to make a buck.

When I asked Harvey Mackay what made him such a blend of highly competitive CEO and relational salesman extraordinaire who can swim in any school of sharks unharmed, he said this:

"The fact that my father was a people person. He was one of the best journalists in the St. Paul/Minneapolis area and won national journalistic awards, as well as the Humanitarian of the Year award.

"Being in that atmosphere and growing up with that, my dad let me know that from the human aspect it didn't matter who it was, he would talk to everyone and he was friendly with everyone.

There was no difference between the governor, whom he was close to, and the person who shined his shoes."

During our conversation, Mackay noted that hardly a week goes by that he doesn't mention his dad and his influence upon his life. Jack Mackay was never wealthy by monetary standards, but he was rich beyond measure where it really counted—in relationships. He left his son a legacy that lived long after he passed away in 1969.

You'll make plenty of sales if you build relationships by remembering Harvey Mackay's motto: People don't care how much you *know* about them once they realize how much you *care* about them. People detect when you really care, so mark it down:

LEMAN'S LAW #14:

Don't just try to make a sale, make a friend.

A recent report from J. D. Power and Associates says the number of auto saleswomen is growing fast and they are out-scoring the men with their honesty, sincerity, and concern as they deal with their customers.

Granted, many of the votes for female sales persons come from women customers, who do the buying of almost half of all new cars, according to the Power's report. Women, it appears, relate better to women who are buying cars, probably because of their softer-sell approach, which is going over better these days. Also, because they are in a male-dominated field, they just plain work harder to prove themselves.

According to Power and Associates, out of 184,000 people in new car sales, only 25,000 are women. One of these is Londa Schrager, who sells cars for a Lincoln-Mercury dealer in New

York State. She says, "Do I relate better to women? I don't know. I relate well to people. I think a woman salesperson just does a little bit more."[5]

For men or women, Londa has a good word to the wise: Do a little bit more. Relate to your customers. Sales are sure to follow.

The Bottom Line

1. How important is building relationships in my sales strategy? What can I look back on during this past month that is proof of that importance?

2. How do I feel about trying to position myself as Number Two? Am I Number Two with any potential clients right now?

3. Are short notes something I could use more? To whom could I drop a short note right now?

4. Do I build relationships just to make sales or is there something more? How many of my customers or other business colleagues could I count as friends at any level?

PART III

Be a Birth Order Manager and Do a Better Job

Winning the business rat race without be-coming a rat isn't really about percentages, product mix, or P&L sheets. These are important, of course, but above all that, way above, are people. It always comes back to people . . . getting behind their eyes and learning to understand how they think, realizing they want to be treated as unique individuals.

CHAPTER SEVEN

Your Plane Is Taxiing for Takeoff— Is Your Pilot a First Born?

Being a boss, manager, or employer is easy. All you need to answer are three simple questions:

1. How can I get good people?
2. How do I keep them?
3. How do I make a little money in the process?

Everywhere I go I hear business people talking about these problems. I sit next to them on airplanes and watch them as they plow through the latest issue of *Forbes* or *Business Week*, or perhaps it's the latest business guru's best-seller explaining cross-training, symbiosis, and why downsizing is a form of self-cannibalization.

With all these heavy terms dancing through their heads, I understand why business people don't spend a lot of time thinking about birth order. But as we dig into this section on management, I hope you won't sell it short. If you take the time to understand the basics, it is my immodest contention that it could mean the difference between having a so-so year or a great year; it could even mean saving your job instead of spending the next six to twelve months with résumé in hand trying to find another one.

Speaking of résumés, here's what Bruce Dingman, president of the Dingman Company, which specializes in executive search consultant work, says about birth order:

Your insights have meant so much to me I just had to write. About six years ago I read *The Birth Order Book* and since then I've used it as instructions and signs to watch for when trying to understand candidates for positions I am trying to fill. I don't assume someone has to be just as the book suggests, but I watch for the tendencies to be so. . . . Thank you for the wisdom you impart in your books. I appreciate it.

Because I don't make a major project out of saving "testimonial letters," I often mentally file away comments I hear executives make about how they use birth order. In one case, I thought I remembered something Michael C. Feiner, a former senior vice-president at Pepsico Europe, said about birth order. As I began working on this book, I dropped him a note to check on what I thought he said, and here is his reply:

Your memory serves you well with respect to my closing question during an interview [of a prospective employee]. I usually ask one last question: "Can you tell me about your personal background—parents, siblings?" Then I just listen as tons of information begin to pour from the candidate. . . . This is the richest part of the interview in terms of learning about the candidate and the defining moments of his/her personal life.

There is no question that the birth order principle is a principle that I agree with and believe in. Because getting things done in a large complex organization is so dependent on relationships, I probe quite extensively about family relationships and how the candidate carved out his/her own turf with his/her family.

During an interview [of a prospective employee], I usually ask one last question: "Can you tell me about your personal background—parents, siblings?" Then I just listen as tons of information begin to pour from the candidate.
—Michael C. Feiner,
*Former Senior Vice-President,
Pepsico Europe*

Why Are There So Many "Bad Hires"?

According to one specialist in the hiring and interviewing process, "A Labor Department study shows that fifty percent of new hires last only six months in their new jobs." The same specialist believes that the cause of any bad hire can be traced to several reasons, including poor analysis of job functions, poor analysis of necessary personality skill profile, and inadequate questioning techniques.[1]

I believe another big reason for bad hires is that employers don't bother to know that much about the candidate's background. That's why asking some simple questions about the candidate's family and where and how he or she grew up is so useful. Your goal should be:

*R*otten wood cannot be carved.
—*Harvey Mackay, Chairman and CEO, Mackay Envelope Corporation*

LEMAN'S LAW #15:

Hire character, not characters.

I've always had a saying in my counseling practice when describing the possibilities for a client to make a change in behavior, but not necessarily in basic personality: "The grain of the wood is set, but it can be reshaped." Of course, it helps if the wood is solid. As Harvey Mackay told me: "Rotten wood cannot be carved."

The bottom line to all this philosophy is that it helps to look for character traits like integrity and honesty, not to mention willingness to work hard, just as much as skills, abilities, and training—all of which are emphasized in any résumé.

Something else to remember is that interviewing and hiring is a two-way street. Not only do companies fail to learn enough about the candidates, but the candidates fail to learn enough about the company. It's especially important for a company to let the candidate know what is required. A prime example is United Parcel Service, which is famous for its ads about "running a tight ship."

A lot of ads are fluff or just plain drivel, but in the case of UPS, they mean just what they say. They *do* run a tight ship, and the people who work for them are well trained and well paid as a rule. At the same time, much is expected of UPS personnel, and they come on board knowing they had better be dedicated to the company and be prepared to work long hours.

Take a Page from Lute Olson's Recruiting Manual

Businesses large and small could profit from looking at how some coaches and general managers of athletic teams do recruiting. They want players with great talent, of course, but they also look for character, and sometimes if the character isn't there, they are willing to let the talent go.

Such is the case with Lute Olson, head coach of the University of Arizona basketball Wildcats who are usually right at the top of the Pac-10 heap. Lute has guided the Wildcats to eleven consecutive NCAA postseason appearances, including trips to the Final Four in 1988 and 1994. He has also been named Pac-10 Coach of the Year four times. Since arriving at the U of A in 1983, his teams have been among the nation's best in terms of winning percentages.

As a season ticket holder to most Wildcat sports events, I enjoy watching Lute guide his teams to victory year after year. While talking with Lute about this book, I mentioned, "We've had some of your former players in our home for dinner, and Sande and I have always been impressed by their attitude and manners:

'Mrs. Leman, can I help you clear the table?' I've got to tell you, those kinds of kids are a joy to be around—they really are."

I went on to ask Lute just how he found these kids who could play ball and be gentlemen, too, and as he described his philosophy of recruiting, he mentioned an incident that happened at another university several years before he came to Arizona.

"Actually we had some kids that we would not recruit who ended up playing in the NBA," Lute explained. "We want input from our players on every recruit, and what actually happened is that this kid came in, as all the kids do on a Friday for the visit. We take them on campus and meet with the academic people and then we take them out to dinner with student hosts and the coaching staff. We had three of our players with us, and this particular recruit was so obnoxious to the waitress, so demanding, as if all she had to do was to take care of him personally.

"One of my players came over and just sort of whispered to me, 'Do you mind if we just take him outside and talk to him for a second?' I said that was fine. In essence, they took him outside and said, 'Look, this is not the way the players in our program respond. We don't want this kind of thing reflecting on our program, so just shape up or don't look at this as a possibility for you.'"

According to the rest of the story, the recruit improved a little bit for the rest of the evening but not enough to impress the three players or the coaching staff. They all met the next morning and agreed that this particular young man wasn't going to fit in the program.

You might think that with these high standards, Lute Olson would have all kinds of rules that he lays on his players, but as we talked he said, "We don't set down a whole lot of rules. We have probably the fewest rules that you'd ever want to have. *The rule* is don't ever do anything that would embarrass you, your teammates, or the program.

That covers a gamut of things and applies to their academics, how they appear in class, what they do in the community. We know that they are college-age kids and they are going to make mistakes, but as long as they understand what our basic rule is, we're okay."

The thing that strikes me about *the rule* is that it can apply across the board—to four-year-olds, junior college transfers, drill-press operators, receptionists, or vice-presidents of marketing. In fact, I like Lute's rule so much I'd like to paraphrase it just a bit:

LEMAN'S LAW #16:

Never do anything that would embarrass you, your fellow workers, or your company.

Lute Olson's approach to recruiting is the same one that we've always had at the University of Arizona over the years. When I was working on my master's and doctorate at the U of A, I was a head resident in one of the athletic dorms—that is, where the athletes stayed. I lived with these kids and pretty well knew all about them. Members of the coaching staff would constantly be stopping me to ask about certain kids: "How did he keep his room? Did I know if he went to class? Had he ever been in any trouble? Did he smoke any dope?"

It always impressed me that all of these questions were centered on the students' lifestyles. The coaches knew what the young men could do out on the athletic field or on the court, but they didn't know what they were doing back in their dorms or on campus.

I know some people have a very jaded opinion of student athletes, and they might smile a bit at our obsession with morals and character at the U of A. After all, they don't *have* to graduate.

If they're any good, the pro teams will snatch them up no matter how they might live off the field, right?

Not necessarily. A few years ago, the late Richie McCabe, former backfield coach for the Denver Broncos, was in Tucson to look over some of the Wildcat football players. As I sat with my friend at Arizona Stadium watching the team work out, he kept asking me about the kids. To my surprise, most of Richie's questions weren't directed at their stats or what they could do in certain game situations. Instead, he kept inquiring about personal habits, attitudes—What kind of kids were they off the field?

*T*here are a lot of really good football players all over this country. But there are very few who can play on Sunday afternoon.
—*Richie McCabe,*
former Denver Bronco
backfield coach

This coach for the Denver Broncos was asking the same questions our coaches always asked. I told McCabe what I knew about certain players' personal habits and lifestyles, but at one point I must confess I slipped into throwing in a few raves about a particular linebacker who was a truly outstanding football player. As I began telling him about some of this kid's exploits, he held up a hand and said, "Kevin, there are a lot of really good football players all over this country. But there are very few who can play on Sunday afternoon."

What Richie McCabe was saying is that many want to be drafted but few are chosen for very good reasons. The pro teams—the Denver Broncos, at least—don't just recruit talent or ability; they recruit character and integrity because they know it pays off down the line.

The moral is obvious. You really can't be too careful when you're hiring someone. Every CEO, superintendent, or manager must understand that an organization is only as good as the people who represent that organization.

Pat Williams, general manager of the NBA basketball pow-erhouse, the Orlando Magic, agrees. When I asked him if he had had to fire many people over the years, he said, "I've had to do it a few times and I hated it. That's why I've become committed to hiring the right people. I've always done careful and thorough research and just worked at doing everything possible to get the right people in place. I would rather walk on hot coals than fire somebody. It's the worst thing in the world. I despise it so much I made the decision to do everything in my power to find the right person for each job."

You really can't be too careful when you're hiring someone. . . . An organization is only as good as the people who represent that organization.

As important as finding good character is, there is one other very practical issue, and, as you might sus-pect, birth order comes into play in a big way. That issue is finding the right people for the right job.

Try to Put the Right Combinations Together

To give you a graphic example, all I have to do is take to the friendly skies. Because my speaking assignments take me to all corners of the U.S. and into Canada, I do a *lot* of flying. If I'm on the plane just a few minutes before takeoff, I like to work my way up front to where the pilots usually have their cockpit door open, watching people file on board. As I go by, I pop my head in and ask them just one question: "How are all the first borns today?"

Before any of them can react, I go back to my seat and wait to see if they will take the bait. About seven times out of ten, one of the flight crew will work his way back to me before takeoff and say something to the effect: "Uh, are you the gentleman who said something about first borns? Why did you ask us that?"

"Well, you're all first borns up front there in the cockpit, aren't you?" I reply, assuming that they couldn't possibly be anything else.

Far more often than not, the answer is, "As a matter of fact, we are."

I don't take time at this point to give the person a short birth order lecture. I just smile and say, "Good, because if all three of you were babies of the family, I'm out of here!"

At this point the pilot works his way back to the front to prepare for takeoff, shaking his head and muttering things about "the interesting people who fly the friendly skies."

I give my first-born greeting to airline pilots partly for fun but also to confirm what I have seen again and again among the first borns of this world. They are meticulous, perfectionistic, precise individuals who are often in positions of leadership, such as commanding airliners. I'm not saying that a last born can't be a good airline pilot; occasionally, my informal "poll" turns one up, but what I am saying is this:

1. I don't find many last borns piloting airliners or even working as a number two– or three–man in the cockpit. Out of one hundred pilots I informally surveyed, ninety-eight men and two women, 88 percent were first borns or only borns in their families.

2. All things being equal, with first borns in the cockpit, I—a typical fun-loving, not-too-worried-about-details last born— feel safer because first borns *hate to fail*, and first borns *must* do things right.

The Day I Almost Bailed Out

On one occasion, however, my polling of airline pilots appeared to backfire in my face. My colleague Randy Carlson and

I were on our way to do a parenting seminar and we had just squeezed on a little commuter plane about to take off from L.A., destination Santa Maria, 140 miles up the California coast. If you've ever ridden one of these little commuters, you know how small they are—one narrow row of seats on one side, a very narrow aisle, and a narrow row of seats on the other.

We wound up right up front by the door to the cockpit which, in these small commuters, is almost always open or nonexistent. Because we were three feet from the two guys flying the plane, it was easy to notice the lead pilot's digital watch.

"You're a first born, aren't you?" I said comfortably.

"No, actually, I'm a baby of the family," he replied.

"How about your buddy?" I said, beginning to get a bit nervous.

He leaned over, conversed briefly with his copilot, turned and said, "He's the youngest too!"

We had two babies flying our little commuter plane and we were practically taxiing for takeoff! I looked at Randy and he looked at me. "Randy," I said, "I think I'm getting off right now and taking a cab the 140 miles up to Santa Maria."

Because Randy has done many seminars with me, he's used to minor crises, so he said calmly to the lead pilot, "Tell me, is there a big gap between you and the next oldest child in your family?"

"Yeah, about twelve years," came the reply.

I slumped back in relief, muttering to Randy, "Okay, with a gap like that, he's more like a first born than a baby. Maybe I'll stay."

Then Randy nudged the copilot and asked the same question. It turned out that there was a six-year gap between him and his older brother, who was a pilot as well!

That settled it. The law of variables said we had a couple of first-born types for pilots because they had been born so far from the next oldest siblings.

The postscript to the story is that we made it to Santa Maria quite nicely, thank you, and both of our last-born pilots did a beautiful job, even when the air got a little rough. In fact, allowing for "the rule of the variable," these two guys would definitely wind up in the 88th percentile of my informal survey that proved most pilots were first borns or only borns in their families.

That the vast majority of pilots I surveyed were first borns, or people with many first-born traits, demonstrates a key point that I'm trying to make: *Some birth orders are better fitted to certain jobs than others.* And, of course, it follows that it is not best to put certain birth orders together on certain jobs—for example, the cockpit of an airliner.

Suppose, for example, the lead pilot of our commuter plane had been paired with a real baby of the family like me? To put it another way, traits like *meticulous* and *exacting* don't go very well with characteristics like *casual, happy-go-lucky*, and even *sloppy*. To say we're "On the money" is a lot different from saying, "Close enough, I guess."

Am I saying, then, that you can never mix birth orders on the job? No, all I'm trying to emphasize is you *must* mix them carefully and, in some cases, vastly different personalities can complement each other and make for harmony and better effectiveness.

Debbie Keeps Me Organized—Sort Of

For example, I'm a last born and the president of my firm, which specializes in psychology, counseling, consulting, and inspirational speaking. Whenever I hire anyone to assist me—someone to run my office, that is—do I look for a charming last-born baby who loves to have fun and isn't too worried about schedules, timing, or dates? No, I look for a first born who is worried about all those things and more.

My assistant and office manager, Debbie Backus, is a first-born diamond I found here in the rough deserts of Tucson who keeps me organized and out of trouble, that is, when I bother to read all her notes, lists, and other reminders.

Being a baby, I love toys and gadgets, and one piece of hardware that I've purchased to help me stay on the straight and narrow is a tiny little shirt-pocket-size computer called a Digital Diary. Described as a calculator, a calendar, and a notebook all in one, my Digital Diary is a wonderful little tool. But the one who really makes it all work is Debbie. She's constantly typing on it to fill in information that I need, particularly my appointments for the next day, the next week, and so forth.

In addition, Debbie relies on something as old-fashioned as a little scrap of paper about the size of a telephone message pad that contains my "game plan" for the next day. I get this every night before I leave, and Debbie can only hope that somewhere between the scrap of paper and my Digital Diary I will get where I'm supposed to be the next day.

Unfortunately, I often stick the scrap of paper in my pocket and forget it. And I'm afraid I don't always look at my Digital Diary as often as I should. That happened not too long ago, and I wound up forty-five minutes late for a taping session with my "Parent Talk" colleagues. But Debbie keeps trying, and so do I. Without Debbie to keep me focused on our immediate goals, I'd be in *big* trouble. The point: Debbie, the first born, and Cub, the irrepressible baby, make a good team.

How One Successful Retailer Picks Her People

Among the business people I interviewed for this book was Delores Maddox, owner and general manager of Gospel Supplies

Christian Book Retailer, which has two stores in the Tucson area. I've known Delores for years and we always have a great time talking—could it be because we're both last-born babies of the family? While working on this chapter I dropped in on her to get some of her insights on how she hires and manages people. Following is a transcript of our interview:

Kevin: How do you put together a good team in the retail business?

Delores: You want mostly babies and second borns out on the floor, selling to customers. We have a few first borns who sell, but most of them are in back in management, accounting, or in the stockroom—behind the scenes.

Kevin: Give me your insights on first-born children in the marketplace. How do you see them working in or running a business?

Delores: From what I've seen of how first borns run businesses, they don't have a lot of variety in their personality and approach. They usually key in on one thing and they do that one thing. I've also noticed they're impatient. In the book-selling market you often have to make changes—in inventory particularly. Usually we have about a two-month lag time, and this drives my first-born people crazy. They want to change everything right now. So, I have to be more patient with the first borns on my staff. But I do listen to them because they have incredible input.

Kevin: Compare first borns and last borns for me. What are their strengths and weaknesses in your opinion?

Delores: First borns are consistent. They're here on time, in fact, they're here early. And they follow through;

they're great finishers. Babies don't like to finish things. They are great starters—they start all these fires and they get people pumped up but somebody else has to finish.

Kevin: You just mentioned some first-born strengths— what are some of their weaknesses?

Delores: I get impatient with first borns because they're not flexible enough. They tend to be single-minded, good at doing one thing at a time. Later borns, on the other hand, especially babies, are able to juggle things much better.

Kevin: Can you give me a couple of examples of how this first-born inflexibility shows itself in day-to-day operations?

Delores: When we get really busy, I may have to ask a first-born sales person to shift from one area to another. This often throws the first-born employee for a loop because he or she thinks, "I have to know everything about that other department or I can't work there." The babies, on the other hand, simply want to know, "Where are the customers? Let me at 'em!"

Another real problem I have with my first-born sales people is that when we train them for retail work, we give them our rule book. We have procedures that are supposed to be followed. The trouble with first borns is that they believe rules are rules and they're not to be broken or even bent.

Kevin: For instance?

Delores: Suppose someone comes in to exchange a gift or a book but they have no receipt. My first-born sales people simply don't bend because our policy says, "No exchanges or refunds without a receipt." I have a hard time getting through to them that it's more important to maintain a good relationship with the customer than to enforce all the rules. If the item is undamaged and it's something we can put right back into stock, a receipt isn't really that important in that case. Then it's time to bend.

Kevin: I remember once you told me that the only first born you had on board was the bookkeeper.

Delores: That's when we were smaller and had about ten people, 80 percent of whom were babies of the family. Now we have thirty-two people and the breakdown is: Eight first borns or only children, eight middle children, and sixteen babies. Most of our last borns are out on the floor selling, as you might well guess.

Kevin: Do you have any observances about middle children on your staff?

Delores: We have several, and I find that you have to drive them, push them. But if you have a problem, they just kind of "go with the flow." They're great.

Kevin: What about hiring? Do you have a set way that you sit down and talk with someone looking for a job?

Delores: Yes, we do. We give a TIMS test, which is a Myers-Briggs type of test.

Kevin: What does a test like that do for you?

Delores: Well, for one thing it tells us if the position we're planning to put the person in is going to energize him or her or if it's going to suck the person dry. According to Myers-Briggs, as a rule, introverts get sucked dry by having to deal with a lot of people while extroverts get turned on and energized by people. Put the wrong person out there on the floor dealing with a lot of people and they'll only be with you for six months because they can't handle it anymore.

Kevin: One of my first observations of your store as I walk in is that this is a place where people would want to spend time. Obviously, this has to be one of your goals—to keep people in the store. Everywhere they turn they can see products they might be interested in buying.

Delores: We have quality recordings playing in the background, and that helps them want to stay, but I really believe it's our people. In retail you have to be emotionally attached to the customer. You have to think like the customer thinks in order to know what the customer wants. And that's another strength of our sales force, which is made up mostly of last borns. Babies tend to be practical— they had to learn to be practical in order to survive growing up. The more practical you are, the better it is for retail sales.

Talking to Delores Maddox shows that birth order knowledge applies differently in different settings. She clearly tries to keep different birth orders working in their respective areas of strength in her retail operation. But are there any occupations where different birth orders could be paired *together* and still do a great job? Absolutely, and all you have to do is turn on your TV set any morning of the week to find out.

What Do the "Big Three" Morning Shows Have in Common?

On different occasions, I've been a guest on all three network morning newscasts—*Good Morning, America, The Today Show,* and *CBS Good Morning*. I believe it's no coincidence that the hosts on all three of these shows are interesting blends of baby and first-born personalities.

Now I am sure that a group of bigwigs at NBC, CBS, or ABC didn't sit down and decide to go find hosts with complementary birth orders. But that's just what happened. For example, for years at CBS, the lovely, exacting Paula Zahn, a first-born perfection-istic player of the cello, was teamed with fun-loving Harry Smith, a baby of the family.

At NBC, engaging Katie Couric, baby of the family, is matched with immaculate Bryant Gumbel, the second born of two brothers who, somewhere along the way, picked up a number of first-born characteristics, including impeccable dress, being suavely aggressive, and a perfectionist of the first order.

I'm not sure what variable kicked in with Bryant—it wasn't a complete role reversal because his big brother, Greg, has made his mark in broadcasting as well. As I have pointed out, the second born of two is hard to figure. The bottom line is that on *The Today Show*, you have a charming baby princess and a super-capable prince (with many first-born personality traits) who match each other nicely.

Over at ABC, which I admit is my favorite, who do we have on top-rated *Good Morning, America*? Charles Gibson is an easy-going, engaging last born who is teamed with the beautiful and hard-driving Joan Lunden, only daughter in her family. Of all three network teams, Charlie and Joan act on the air the "most opposite" of their birth orders. At times, Joan's charming ways make you think she might be a last born, while Charlie's relaxed but confident in-charge manner suggests that he could be a first born.

In fact, Gibson has a hard time deciding if he wants to be "Charles" or "Charlie," and often refers to himself by either name. The mystery is solved, however, when we learn that Charlie is a baby of the family, who is twelve years away from his next older sibling. While he grew up as the family mascot, he received plenty of first-born characteristics because his siblings were so much older and more capable models for him.

If you're interested in hiring good people, keeping them, and making a little money, too, remember the two points made in this chapter:

1. Hire people with character, not characters who bring all their baggage with them.

2. Try matching the personality of the person you are hiring with the job he or she is supposed to do.

Also, try looking ahead to see how this person will match up with other people on your business team. A key birth order principle usually proves itself out over the long run in any organization:

LEMAN'S LAW #17:

Always try to put the right people together, with certain birth orders complementing the strengths or weaknesses of others.

Next we will look at a certain kind of employee who must be carefully matched with those he works with or those he manages. I'm talking about the perfectionists, those driven individuals who can settle for nothing but perfect work every time. You may have perfectionists working for you, or you may be one yourself. To many people, perfectionism seems to be a positive trait, but actually it is a dangerous disease that can cost your company buckets of money every year. In Chapter Eight, I'll explain why.

The Bottom Line

1. In my business, do I hire character first or is ability my main concern?

2. Am I trying to put together a *team* or do I have *individuals* who rub each other (and me) the wrong way?

3. Do I know who I've hired (or am hiring)? Do I take the time to get to know them with a relational approach?

4. Do I have any idea concerning the birth orders of those I direct or manage? Have I thought about who is in the right/wrong spot and what I can do to shift people around, if possible?

CHAPTER EIGHT

How to Manage Perfectionists (Yourself Included)

I n earlier chapters, I made different comments about the dangers of perfectionism, a trait that is usually found in only children and other first-born personalities. That doesn't mean, however, that middle children and even last-born babies can't succumb to the perfectionist "virus."

Obviously, perfectionism isn't really caused by a virus, but it is a form of behavior that can be so pervasive and destructive in one's personality that it causes enough stress to severely handicap or even incapacitate some people. To put it simply:

LEMAN'S LAW #18:

Perfectionism is slow suicide.

By far, the majority of clients I treat for extreme perfectionism are first borns, because they had only adults for models during those early formative years. These adults were almost always Mom and Dad, who seemed so big, so powerful, and so perfect in every way. Later-born children are less perfectionistic because they benefited from the presence of older brothers and sisters, whose behavior was much less "perfect" than their parents'.

If a later-born child turns out to be a perfectionist, it's a first-born characteristic that he or she got from somewhere, depending on certain variables that were at work.

As dangerous as perfectionism can be, a lot of people don't

see it as that much of a threat. In fact, I often have clients tell me, "C'mon, Doc, a little perfectionism is good. The world could use a few more perfectionists instead of accepting all of the sloppy, slipshod work and service that go on every day."

My response is that perfectionism isn't like getting pregnant. You can't be "a little bit" pregnant, but you can be *moderately* perfectionistic, *very* perfectionistic, or *extremely* perfectionistic.

It's the "very" and "extreme" categories that I'm particularly concerned about. *Extreme perfectionism* is an obsessive-compulsive drive within many people that demands that they do an absolutely flawless job *every time* with no mistakes, no errors, no glitches, no foul-ups, not even a burp or a hiccup.

How Perfectionistic Are You?

To see how much of a perfectionist you are, take the following quiz. Just fill in the blank next to each question with 0 for never, 1 for seldom, 2 for often, and 3 for always. Then add up your score.

___ 1. Do mistakes—your own or others'—irritate you?

___ 2. Do you feel everyone should be as driven to do his best as you are?

___ 3. Do you use the word *should* a lot—as in "I should have taken care of that" or "We should meet on this immediately"?

___ 4. Do you find it hard to enjoy success? Even when something goes well, is it easy for you to find the things that could have been just a little better?

___ 5. Does one small mistake ruin your day—or at least your morning?

___ 6. Do terms like *good enough* and *just about right* bother you, particularly on the job?

___ 7. Do you tend to put things off because you feel you're not quite ready to do the job right?

___ 8. Do you find yourself apologizing for certain work because you could have done it better if you "had had more time"?

___ 9. Whether in a meeting, working in a team, or in any group situation in the workplace, do you prefer to be in control of what's happening?

___ 10. Realizing your deep need to have all your ducks in a row, do you insist that those around you have their ducks in the same row (think exactly the way you do)?

___ 11. Do you tend to see the glass half empty instead of half full?

Scoring:

11-16—mild perfectionist

17-25—medium perfectionist

26-33—extreme perfectionist (you're too hard on yourself and everyone else)

If you're in the medium-to-extreme range of perfectionism, you need to ask yourself one more question: "Do I feel guilty much of the time?" For most perfectionists, the answer is "Yes." The more perfectionistic a person is, the more guilt he or she will carry. That guilt surfaces to reveal two different kinds of perfectionists: defeated and discouraged.

Defeated Perfectionists Are Hard on Everybody

Extreme perfectionists who fall into the category of "defeated," can become extremely critical of themselves and others, hiding their coldblooded pursuit of perfection behind the mask of "being objective." They simply will not tolerate mistakes or failures by themselves or by those who work with them or for them. They often have a little desk plaque that reads: "The good is the enemy of the best!"

The defeated perfectionist can be so critical of himself and others that he becomes a constant irritant. He can even become toxic or dangerous, getting fellow workers so angry or so worried about their performance that they can't function properly or safely.

If you have this kind of defeated perfectionist on your payroll and he is in a position where he can directly affect the work of other people, you may want to consider strong measures. Obviously, your first approach is to give this person a chance to change and to modify his behavior, but if the extreme perfectionism continues, your best option is to consider transferring him to another area—or suggest that he look for another line of work.

On the other hand, suppose you are working for a defeated perfectionist (for example, the president or owner of the company). Be aware that if you are in the hands of a truly extreme, defeated perfectionist, you will never please this person. He or she will constantly be hammering you with the negative and giving very little by way of positive reinforcement. Perhaps the financial return for your job will make it worth it to stay, but if self-fulfillment and job satisfaction are truly important to you, you may want to consider working somewhere else.

Discouraged Perfectionists Usually Attack Themselves

Some extreme perfectionists, on the other hand, don't attack others as much as themselves. Often these folks don't think they fit the perfectionist category at all. Their desks are piled so high nobody comes near because they don't want to die in an avalanche. Their motto may be, "A creative mess is better than tidy idleness."

Other signs of discouraged perfectionism can be difficulty in getting started, always being behind schedule, and being tired, "just plain tired."

All of the above are signs of discouraged perfectionism. Just because
you're messy doesn't mean you're not
a perfectionist. You started out in life
wanting to be perfect, probably wanting to please a perfect mom or dad,

*P*erfectionism is slow suicide. . . . At the very least, perfectionists can easily burn out.

but along the way you became so frustrated you've given up on things. So you plug along, feeling even more guilt and more frustration with your untidy, sloppy, or procrastinating ways.

When I work with discouraged perfectionists, I often have them do a simple exercise. On one side of a sheet of paper I ask them to list characteristics that describe what they might call "the ideal self"—the kind of person they would like others to see all the time. On the other side of the sheet I ask them to list characteristics that describe their "real self"—the kind of person they actually are. The result is that the "ideal me" is often a far cry from the "real me."

For example, ideally the perfectionist would want to be "orga-nized, efficient, with no wasted motion." But what about the "real me"? The discouraged perfectionist usually puts down things like "disorganized, inefficient, seem to be spinning my wheels much of the time."

When perfectionists can't meet the "ideal me" goals, they feel dissonance and disjointedness. In fact, the more difference there is between one's ideal description of oneself and "the real me," the more dissonance and dysfunction there will be. I have discour-aged perfectionists do this exercise because I want to help them see that their unreachable goals make them sitting ducks for disappointment.

Discouraged perfectionists aren't always easy for a manager

to spot. You may have discouraged perfectionists under your leadership who are super pleasers, anxious to solve everyone's problems. They may even be looked upon as "heroes" or "heroines" because of their ability to move in, take over, and rescue whoever needs rescuing or solve whatever needs solving. This may be fine in the short run. These pleaser-perfectionists don't do damage to fellow workers, in fact, they usually help and are often labeled, "indispensable," or are described in terms such as, "What would we do without him [or her]?"

But Leman's Law still holds: "Perfectionism is slow suicide." Be aware that discouraged pleaser-perfectionists can slowly but surely destroy themselves. At the very least, they can easily burn out, as they carry everyone else's burdens along with their own.

The Perfectionist's Road to Defeat

If you scored twenty or above on the perfectionist's quiz, you should take a careful look at the following "cycle of perfectionism" that can lead you straight down the road to defeat.[1] And if you scored lower on the perfectionist's quiz and feel it's no problem for you, keep in mind that it probably is a problem for certain people on your staff or in your company. You need to know how to recognize perfectionism in the people you manage because it will help you understand them and how to deal with them better.

1. *Perfectionists are sure they must be perfect.* Whatever they do, their motto is "It's all or nothing."

2. *Perfectionists bite off more than they can chew.* This is just about every perfectionist's biggest problem. They believe they can always take on one more thing, finish one more project ahead

of schedule, and so forth. The trouble is, they can't, and it leads to the next step toward defeat.

3. *Panic sets in.* In psychological terms, the "hurdle effect" takes over. They look down the track and see all those hurdles ahead—each one a little higher than the last. All these perceived obstacles appear to be too much, and they are sure they face defeat. They wring their hands, saying, "How did I get into this? And how will I ever get out?"

4. *Perfectionists continue to make things worse by maximizing their failures and minimizing their successes.* Instead of learning from their mistakes, they internalize them. If they do something right, they tend to depreciate it with this famous line: "It could have been a lot better."

5. *Perfectionists often bail out early.* In other words, they may quit a project or turn it in half-done, giving the excuse that "I simply didn't have enough time."

6. *Perfectionists constantly vow to "try harder."* Instead of believing they have worth because of who they are, they are convinced that they "are what they do." The joker in this deck is that they can never do enough and they are never satisfied.

The bad news about these six steps is that, for the perfectionist who doesn't seek to change, this cycle is repeated over and over, often several times a day. The trouble is, perfectionists have real difficulty with changing anything. Their lockstep, black-and-white, no-gray-area approach to life keeps them bogged down in their same cycle. The good news, however, is that, if they want to make the effort, they can control their relentless pursuit of perfectionism and even turn it into a much healthier direction—seeking excellence.

How to Move from Perfectionism Toward Excellence

If you are a medium to extreme perfectionist, you may be thinking, *Okay, I admit it. I'm a perfectionist. What am I supposed to do—shoot for being so-so or inferior?*

A lot of my clients say the same thing (a sure sign that they're perfectionists). The perfectionist thinks that if he isn't striving every second to be the absolute best there is, he has to settle for the other extreme of mediocre or lousy. There is, however, a great middle ground between flawlessness and mediocrity where perfectionists can find happiness *if they're willing to work on their problem*.

The first step is to confess that you are, indeed, a perfectionist. Deep down you must be ready to admit that perfectionism drives your life too hard and you need to do something about it.

Your second step is to make a conscious decision to use what I call cognitive discipline to change how you look at things. Stop and assess the situation. Ask yourself, "What do I usually do? How am I going to do this differently to avoid the perfectionistic trap?"

The key is to recognize when you are going on "perfectionist autopilot" and to break the cycle. Go back and review the cycle again. Two of the best places to use cognitive discipline are on Steps 1 and 2. Instead of telling yourself, "It's all or nothing," and then biting off more than you can chew, remind yourself, "It doesn't have to be all or nothing; how much of this project can I do without putting myself in the same old bind?"

If you *do* bite off more than you can chew and *realize it*, rejoice! Just admitting to yourself that you know you slipped into your same old perfectionistic ways is a victory. Next time, you'll be able to think it through a little better and make wiser choices.

With practice, you'll be able to recognize when you start to go on autopilot into the same old habits. If you're a football fan, refer to it as "calling an audible" at the line of scrimmage; if football is not your thing, just call it "choosing a better option" before the perfectionistic cycle kicks in again.

None of this will be easy, because perfectionists are creatures of habit. They love to stay in their comfort zone, on familiar terrain, in the same routines. The trouble is, today's business climate is getting more and more severe for perfectionists. In these days of cutbacks and downsizings, a giant like AT&T will announce a layoff of forty thousand employees, and it hardly makes a ripple. Perfectionists who want to survive, or possibly even thrive, must suck it up and be willing to step out of their comfort zone, break the perfectionistic cycle, and become more efficient.

Slowly you will move from pursuing perfectionism toward seeking excellence. One (perfectionism) is a form of sickness, the other (excellence) is a healthy way to go about your work.

In the following quiz, pursuers of perfectionism are described in the left column and seekers of excellence are on the right. Take a few minutes and check off the phrases that *seem to come closest* to describing you at this time in your life. If you wind up feeling that "I'm somewhere between these two extremes," check the column that describes the direction in which you seem to lean. Take your time with this exercise and be very honest with yourself. To get full benefit, you need to take a good look inside at who you really are.

Are You Sick or Healthy?

Pursuers of Perfectionism	Seekers of Excellence
____ reach for impossible goals	____ enjoy meeting high standards that are within reach
____ value themselves by what they do	____ value themselves by who they are
____ get depressed and give up	____ learn from failures
____ remember mistakes and dwell on them	____ correct mistakes, then learn from them
____ can only live with being Number One	____ are happy with being Number Two, if they know they have tried their hardest
____ hate criticism	____ welcome criticism
____ have to win to keep high self-esteem	____ finish second and still have a good self-image

To determine your score, check off the descriptions that best describe you. Then add them up to see if you are mostly a pursuer of perfection, mostly a seeker of excellence, or a little bit of both. Remember, be very honest.

The Story of Edwin, Perfectionist-in-Process

To show you how someone can move from perfectionism toward excellence, I want to share with you the story of Edwin, an only child who is an executive with a large computer firm.

Edwin picked up a copy of *The Birth Order Book* several years ago. When he came to the chapter on only children and perfectionism, he knew I had him cold. He wrote to thank me for opening his eyes and helping him understand why he behaved in such compulsive ways. For example, in his closet, dress shirts are on white hangers, and sport shirts are on brown hangers. Oh, yes, darker colored dress shirts are on the *left* and lighter colored dress shirts are on the *right*.

Edwin mentioned several other things that *The Birth Order Book* had shown him. For example, throughout his career his desk had been a mess most of the time, but he could "usually find anything within sixty seconds." Admittedly, however, on occasion he "would lose control" of his desk and become frustrated, angry, or worse.

And, oh, yes, from a favorite aunt (a first born) he learned how to alphabetize the spices in the kitchen cabinet. He closed his letter by saying, "Dr. Leman, you will never know how much enlightenment your book has given me. Thank you."

When I began work on this book, I wrote back to Edwin to see if he'd like to contribute some only-child perfectionist thoughts from a business standpoint. I didn't receive any reply for several months and so I dropped Edwin a line once again. About two weeks later, the following letter arrived. It's not hard to see that Edwin still has some work to do on his perfectionism:

Dear Doc:

Don't panic—I haven't forgotten you.

Gee whiz, I mean, like I have this great job as a VP, and then a good friend who decides to run for Congress asks my boss to loan me to him so I can give him a little help with speech writing, and the boss says OK as long as I do my regular job—and oh, yes, the boss acquires a small software distributing company in the middle of all this and asks yours truly to handle the details (name change, marketing, advertising, and do you have any idea how many things a newly acquired company needs to have its new name printed on?). . . .

. . . and while I'm in the middle of writing the hope-to-be-a-Congressman's most important campaign speech, setting up his press office and dealing with local and national media folks, my company's stock takes a nosedive and the guy who was supposed to install the new signs for the new acquisition calls and says his crew didn't come back from vacation, and Dr. Leman writes me an awfully nice letter asking for help with his new book, and oh sure, I'd be glad to help, so I put that letter in the pile next to the couch. . . .

. . . and, of course, it was during this time that my house-keeper started hanging my dress shirts on the brown hangers instead of the white hangers and Dr. Leman's nice assistant sends me a follow-up letter and I put that in the pile next to the couch as I went out the door to accompany my friend running for Congress to an out-of-state rendezvous with some Party bigwigs who wanted him to change certain campaign strategies, but thank goodness for cellular phones so I could talk one of our large institutional investors out of dumping my company's stock and. . . .

. . . now the friend has won a seat in Congress; the newly acquired company finished a profitable first quarter (the signs were installed at all locations the day before the acquired company opened under its new name); my company's stock is inching upward; I got rid of all the brown hangers and all my shirts are on white ones; and I can now tackle Dr. Leman's request. Stay tuned.

Your fan,
Edwin

One of the most obvious things we can see in Edwin's letter is that he's still biting off more than he can chew by saying yes to life's insatiable demands. At the same time, however, he rather enjoys all of the pressures and stress, which is often true of perfectionists until they start to burn out.

Also note that he is now hanging all his shirts on white hangers after his housekeeper almost ruined his life by getting those hanger colors mixed up! If Edwin ever hires another housekeeper, he needs to ask some obvious birth order questions!

> *I* **used to be easily disappointed and upset when I saw that someone just didn't give 100 percent. Now I realize that, for whatever reasons, not all people have the same motivation.**
> —*Edwin,*
> *A vice-president who is breaking perfectionistic habits*

Finally, after Edwin got through all his crises and had time to "tend to my request," it took him several months before he was able to do so. This suggests that he still has the perfectionist's penchant for procrastination.

But when Edwin did send his answers to my questions, they were, of course, insightful. For example, when I asked him, "You're a vice-president. How do you see your perfectionism helping or hurting you on the job?" he replied:

It helps to strive for perfectionism because you quickly build a reputation for doing quality work. When the boss has an especially important assignment, to whom is he/she going to assign it? That's right, the person who will—based on past experience—do the best job. So, when you get important assignments, and when you do them well, you get noticed . . . and you get promoted.

Early in my career I recall being given a series of assignments. I was not able to complete them in the normal, eight-hour workdays, and put in a considerable amount of noncompensated overtime. I was criticized for this by coworkers. I thought nothing of the additional hours—I simply wanted to do the best possible job I could. I honestly didn't even think about this work leading to a promotion or a raise (which it did). I was just trying to do the best job that I was capable of doing.

Perfectionism hurts, however, because you demand the same (perfection) from your coworkers and subordinates. Occasionally, resentment can result. I used to be easily disappointed and upset when I saw that someone just didn't give 100 percent. Now I realize that, for whatever reasons, not all people have the same motivation.

In the first letter he wrote me, Edwin had claimed he could find anything on his messy desk in sixty seconds, yet he had to admit that at times he would "lose control." In his later letter he mentioned having piles of paper all around his couch, including my request that he couldn't get to for several months. When I asked Edwin if he thought he was making any progress with his messy desk (and couch), he said:

> *Until I read* The Birth Order Book, *I thought that I lost control of my desk because I switched from project to project during the day, putting files on top of other files in a desperate attempt to keep the flow of work moving and not interrupting the momentum by taking time to refile things.*
>
> *However, now I understand that this is merely my defense mechanism to try to convince the world that I am not really a perfectionist. That way I am less likely to be criticized. Only children, you know, don't want to be criticized even if it is for being a perfectionist! And don't criticize me for a messy desk either. I've improved my desk since I've read* The Birth Order Book.

While Edwin believes he has improved his desk, he also obviously still struggles with perfectionism. In fact, when I sent him the Perfectionist Quiz (page 138–39), he scored in the high twenties, which puts him in the area of medium-going-toward-extreme perfectionist.

I also sent Edwin the "Perfectionism vs. Excellence Quiz" (page 146) and the results were most encouraging. Although he still struggles with perfectionism (and always will to some degree), Edwin found himself checking the excellence column far more often than the perfectionist column. And when I asked him where he thought he was today—seeking excellence or pursuing perfection on the job—he wrote back:

> *I seek excellence, not perfection. There is a difference. I strive for excellence, knowing that perfection means flawless.*

Let's say we are considering an acquisition, and time is short. My "briefing report" for the acquisitions group will be thorough and complete—covering all of the research and facts— but it may not be perfect. I may include my hand-drawn charts (I'm a lousy artist), not slick, computer-generated charts; some of the T's may not be crossed, but the information will be correct, thorough, and timely. That will be an excellent report, but not a perfect one.

Edwin's answer suggests that he is making real progress with controlling and even conquering his perfectionism. He knows he has the problem and he is dealing with it. Admittedly, there is often a fine line between pursuing perfection and seeking excellence, and every manager or employer who leans toward perfectionism at all should constantly be aware of the difference.

I think Edwin has struggled long enough with his perfectionism to know that difference. Frankly, if I had a larger operation, I would want to hire Edwin myself. In fact, just about any company would be fortunate to have Edwin as a vice-president or even a CEO. Here's a man who not only does things right, but he knows the difference—that fine balancing point—between pursuing perfectionism and seeking excellence.

Another good example of how to walk the perfectionist/excellence tightrope is a man I've been able to watch "up close" from my sixth-row season seat at McKale Center on the University of Arizona campus. As a basketball coach, he's par excellence; as a leader of young men and his own staff, he has much to teach anyone in a leadership position.

Lute Olson: Role Model for All Managers

If you are managing others in any capacity, a model worth emulating is Lute Olson, head coach of the University of Arizona

Wildcats basketball team, one of the most successful athletic programs in the nation. You don't have to be a rocket scientist to see the parallels between coaching a big-time sports program in college or the pros and managing people in any business setting, whether it's large or small. In fact, the "team approach" is everywhere today in businesses large and small. Lute's approach to working with his players and his assistant coaches is a good example of how any manager of people can and should operate, if he wants to lead his team toward excellence while avoiding the pitfalls of extreme perfectionism.

I have to admit that when Lute came to Arizona in 1984, I was sure he had to be a first born and probably a perfectionist to boot. A natty dresser, with beautiful wavy white hair always in place, Olson always looks organized and competent. Frenetic ESPN announcer Dick Vitale loves to kid about Arizona's coach on the air, saying things like, "Lute, Baby! You're far too pretty to be a coach!" But as Vitale and a lot of other people have realized long ago, with Lute Olson, beauty is far more than skin deep.

As I have observed Lute coaching, and as I talk to Wildcat players, I have learned that he is a no-nonsense disciplinarian, but he is not driven by perfectionism.

I've also learned that he is not a first born or an only child. In Lute's case, some very important variables, namely, parental values, came into play and, while Lute may look and act like a first born or only child, he's really the baby of his family! When I talked with Lute about how this could be so, he believed he got his meticulous keep-things-organized-and-everything-in-its-place approach to life from his Scandinavian background.

"I'm Norwegian," he explained, "and it was always a case of at home you were expected to do whatever your job was. You were expected to do it well and there were no excuses accepted for not doing it."

As Lute recalled what it was like growing up on the farm, he told me, "I think that's the way kids were raised in the Midwest at that time; you were expected to give it your best shot."

As Lute went through the "Perfectionism or Excellence" quiz, he came out very much on the side of seeking excellence. He admits that in his U of A basketball program, "Our point here is to reach for the sky. We want to be as good as we can be, but when it's all over and done with, as long as we have played as hard as we can play, and have tried to give it the best effort we can give it, there isn't anything that anybody should expect beyond that."

As for valuing himself by what he does versus valuing himself by who he is, Lute definitely lands in the excellence column, happy with the person he has become. He coached baseball, basketball, and football in several high schools. Then he moved into the college ranks where he concentrated on basketball. From 1969 to 1973 he coached at Long Beach (California) City College, a two-year school. In 1973-74 he was at Long Beach State coaching Division I basketball. From 1974 to 1983 he coached the University of Iowa Hawkeyes, and in 1984 he came to Arizona, where he has been ever since.

Whatever the level, Lute believes, "It really didn't make any difference to me. I've been asked many times, 'When did you set this goal that you wanted to get to Division I?' I never had a goal

> *O*ur point here is to reach for the sky. We want to be as good as we can be, but when it's all over and done with, as long as we have played as hard as we can play, and have tried to give it the best effort we can give it, there isn't anything that anybody should expect beyond that.
> —*Lute Olson,*
> *Head Basketball Coach,*
> *University of Arizona*

to coach basketball in Division I. The whole intent has been trying to do the best job I can do."

How to Fail and Keep Going

As I continued the interview with Coach Olson, I said, "In my counseling I've seen it many times. Perfectionists tend to get depressed and give up. They are also devastated by failure. On the other hand, seekers of excellence may experience disappointment but keep going and learn from their failures."

"My goal is always to be a better coach this year than last," Lute replied. "That has been the way I've tried to do it ever since I started out way back at Mahnomen High School in northern Minnesota. My first year was a good year. The second year my intent was to be more effective and more efficient than the first year. And so it has gone, but to get depressed and give up—obviously you can't do that in coaching."

"But what happens when you lose? And why do you think some players choke in the clutch?"

"The mental part of the game is the hardest for some kids to overcome. For example, a player steps up to the free-throw line with a chance to win or lose the game, and he misses both shots. It's hard for a player to eliminate that from his mind the next time he is in a similar situation. Whether you are a coach or an athlete, you have to be resilient. I take a loss as hard as anybody, but I can't wait to get back at it to make sure that the next game will be different."

As for criticism, Lute Olson believes it all depends where the criticism comes from. He honestly admitted: "I hate criticism when it comes from people who have no clue of what goes into what we do. Now if I'm criticized by someone in the coaching profession that I respect or someone else who knows something about the game, I welcome that criticism and try to straighten out the things that need to be straightened out."

When I asked Lute about learning from mistakes rather than dwelling on them, he had this to say:

"When we lost the Kentucky game last year, I felt really good about how our guys played. There were obviously some things during the course of the game, particularly at the end, if everyone had done his job, it would have been in the win column instead of the loss column. So, we were very happy and pleased with the effort but also aware that there were things that were being done that we needed to do better if we were going to go where we wanted to go."

It's obvious that Lute Olson doesn't have to win to keep his self-esteem in healthy shape. He can finish fifth or second and still have a good self-image, which brings him right back to try again. His players love him and his fans in Tucson do as well. He is in one of the most intense businesses there is—coaching big-time college basketball—but he is handling the stress very nicely, thank you, because he knows the difference between pursuing perfectionism and seeking excellence.

Specific Tips for Seeking Excellence

If you want to seek excellence more and pursue perfectionism less, here are some tips I have gathered from other consultants, as well as those on the business firing lines. The first thing to keep in mind is seeking excellence doesn't mean sloughing off or putting out less effort because it might be "healthier" for you.

One of the best management tapes I've ever heard is "Eleven Keys to Excellence" by leadership consultant John Maxwell. He points out that excellence is not an event but a process. In other words, you don't achieve excellence in one stroke or one week. You work at it over the long haul. Always be aware that the excellent presentation or sales pitch that you will be giving in ten days, ten months, or ten years you are preparing *now* as you do your best on a daily basis.

As for the importance of seeking excellence, Maxwell shares these startling statistics from some of his research:

> If 99.9 percent is good enough, then two million documents will be lost by the IRS this year, twenty-two thousand checks will be deducted from wrong bank accounts in the next sixty minutes, 1,314 telephone calls will be misplaced by TeleCommunications Services every minute, twelve babies will be given to the wrong parents each day . . . over five and a half cases of soft drinks will be produced in the next twelve months that will be flatter than a bad tire, 20,000 incorrect drug prescriptions will be written in the next twelve months—all if 99.9 percent is good enough.[2]

According to Maxwell, one definition of excellence is "going beyond the average." He goes on to say that efficiency means getting the job done right, effectiveness means getting the right job done, but excellence means getting the *right* job done *right*.

One of the best bits of advice Maxwell has for managers is to show genuine respect for others. To make excellence a lifestyle,

Efficiency means getting the job done right. *Effectiveness* means getting the right job done. . . . *Excellence* means getting the right job done right.
—*John Maxwell, Author, Leadership Consultant, and Founder of "INJOY"*

you need to come to the place where you can practice the Golden Rule without giving it a second thought. To do this on the job every day, you must elevate the worth of others to the same level you hold for yourself. But you'll never be able to practice the Golden Rule with your workers if you harbor secret feelings that they are worth less than you are, if deep down you consider them nobodies. If you want to be an excellent manager, value your people. If you want to be a lousy manager, devalue them (more on this in Chapter Eleven and Chapter Twelve).

If reading this chapter has encouraged you to change your perfectionistic ways, go back and review the points on page 146. Keep working on areas where you know you definitely need to make adjustments. Don't expect overnight or immediate improvement (a typical trap for a perfectionist). Instead, expect more of a two-steps-forward-one-step-back kind of progress. But the point is, you can make progress out of perfectionism into seeking excellence, and your boss, your fellow workers, or your employees will love you for it!

The Bottom Line

If you are a perfectionist yourself and want to move toward excellence, tell yourself the following daily—in fact, several times a day:

1. "I understand—and really believe—that no one is perfect."

2. "I understand and really believe that my naturally high standards need to be more reasonable, less excessive."

3. "I'm getting better at really believing that beautiful cathedrals are built one brick at a time, and I need to stay focused until the job is done."

4. "I understand and really believe there are times that I have to depend on the work of others—I can't do it all myself."

5. "When the negative tapes start playing inside my head, I will shut them off and use positive self-talk."

If you have to supervise or manage one or more perfectionists, try using these ideas:

1. Urge perfectionists to take risks, and if they fail say: "We aren't looking for perfection. What we do want to do is learn from our mistakes."

2. When perfectionists finish a project, let them celebrate and savor the victory with them before going on to the next job.

3. Always tell perfectionists they are valued for their attitude—who they are, not "what they do."

4. Always monitor perfectionists to be sure they aren't biting off more than they can chew. If you think they are, encourage them to cut back.

5. When a perfectionist panics, step alongside and help him or her stop and think of what to do next. Probably the best thing is to go out for a cup of coffee and talk it through.

6. When you hear a perfectionist "beating himself up," tell him to stop it—now. Say with a smile, "I don't talk about my people that way and I don't want them to talk about themselves that way either."

CHAPTER NINE

Note to Management: Everyone's Different—Especially Those Last Borns!

I've been reading your books and I'd like to have you talk to my sales staff about how we can move more cars per month."

The voice on the other end of the line belonged to the president of a really big automobile dealership in the heart of Oklahoma. The assignment sounded intriguing so we made a date and a few weeks later I was sitting in his office getting briefed on what he wanted me to accomplish during my visit.

First I heard a lot about how the car business is a really rough way to make a living these days. The margins of 22 to 25 percent are long gone. The factories are making it harder and harder to make a decent profit on a car. And, oh, yes, some of his sales people were giving him problems.

"What kind of problems?" I asked.

"Well, I've got this one guy—he's really a crackerjack salesman, but he never does his paperwork right. I'm thinking about letting him go."

After a few more questions, I learned the following:

1. The president of the dealership was a first born.

2. The salesman who was driving him nuts with lousy paperwork was a baby of the family.

3. This irascible last born who refused to do his paperwork right had been Salesman of the Month at the dealership ten out of the last twelve months.

In short, I had a car dealership president who wanted to fire his best salesman because he didn't do his paperwork right.

All employees are not the same, and you shouldn't try to treat them all alike.

"I think I have the answer to your problem," I told the president. Hire someone else to do this man's paperwork. He's too valuable a salesman to have him bother with those details."

"But I can't do that," the president said. "Dr. Leman, around here I expect everyone to do everything the same way."

"Sir," I replied, "with all due respect, if you insist on that, you have my condolences. All employees are *not* the same, and you shouldn't try to treat them all alike."

Fortunately, the president of the car dealership heard me out. To save face, he set up some new procedures that made paperwork a lot simpler for all of his sales reps. The last-born salesman's job was saved, and I collected a nice check for that one conversation with the president, plus the talk I gave to the entire sales staff on the psychology of selling.

I truly enjoyed my Oklahoma car dealership assignment. For one thing, I've always been fascinated by cars and car sales. Every product has a price, but obviously the sticker price of a car is not the real price. I've always felt that if I had been a car salesman I could have broken records. And I would have enjoyed serving people to get repeat business.

One of the most destructive ideas in business today is, "Everybody around here has to do things the same way." Best-selling business guru Tom Peters is the sworn enemy of the same-way syndrome. In fact, he is so high on urging people to be innovative and creative that he encourages companies to "support past failures." He believes that if companies are to become as innovative as they need to be to survive in today's shark-infested competition, they must *actively encourage failure.*

> *T*o induce constant improvement, *everyone* must be failing faster, including the newest mail clerk, trying to improve his or her method of sorting the mail.
>
> —*Tom Peters,*
> *Author,* Thriving on Chaos

Peters urges companies to get over the "F-word" hurdle, saying: "To induce constant improvement, *everyone* must be failing faster, including the newest mail clerk, trying to improve his or her method of sorting the mail."[1] In his inimitable way, Peters is overstating the case to say that management should encourage its people to take more risks, to try things, and if they fail, not to punish them or hold them hostage on some kind of guilt trip.

By the way, it never hurts for management to flaunt its imperfections and admit its failures as well. If you as a manager want people to approach you, to trust you, and be willing to try taking a few risks themselves, then be open about taking your own risks and admitting your own failures when things don't work. Do all you can to get everyone on your team aware of this bit of business wisdom:

You miss one hundred percent of the shots you never take.[2]

How Birth Order Fits the Team Concept

One reason the "everybody must do it the same" point of view is so dangerous is that it flies in the face of one of the most practical concepts that has hit business circles in years: teamwork. Numerous books have documented the importance of having teams that can produce better results than people working alone.

But there is a funny thing about the team concept. Everyone can't be the quarterback. Everyone can't be a wide receiver. Some people have to do the blocking and the tackling. Obviously, anybody who wants his business to run with good teamwork is shooting himself in the foot if he wants everybody to do things the same way. And when you bring birth order into the mix, you can immediately see that you just don't ask babies of the family to act like first borns. It just isn't in them.

There is a funny thing about the team concept. Everyone can't be the quarterback. Everyone can't be a wide receiver. Some people have to do the blocking and the tackling.

I'm not saying that one birth order is better than another. All of them have their strengths, and the bottom line is that every business team needs *all* the birth orders functioning as a unit to produce the desired results.

In order to get those results, you need to know how to manage each of the birth orders in the most effective way. In earlier chapters, I made a big point over and over: Sales are relational. But really, managing people is no different. The first rule of management is this:

LEMAN'S LAW #19:

Like selling, managing is relational. You have to manage people in a way that is consistent with how they view life.

Winning the business rat race without becoming a rat isn't really about percentages, product mix, or P&L sheets. These are important, of course, but above all that, way above, are people.

It *always* comes back to people—getting behind their eyes, and learning to understand how they think, realizing they want to be treated as unique individuals, according to the Golden Rule.

Everyone Wears an Invisible Sign

If there is anyone in business today who believes in practicing the Golden Rule with her employees and her customers, it is Mary Kay Ash, who started Mary Kay Cosmetics over thirty years ago in a five-hundred-foot storefront and built it into an international multimillion-dollar corporation with a sales force of close to 200,000. Two experiences from Mary Kay's earlier career, before her cosmetics business, made her vow to always treat people as she would want to be treated.

She once spent ten days riding a bus with fifty-seven other sales people all the way from Texas to Massachusetts to be rewarded for being sales leaders in that firm. The bus trip was horrendous, with many breakdowns, but everyone was willing to endure it because they knew they would eventually meet the president of the company and be guests in his home.

Instead, they were given a tour of the plant and when they were finally taken out to the president's home, they were only allowed to walk through his rose garden. Nobody got to meet the president personally. A quiet group of very let-down sales people rode the bus back to Texas.[3]

On another occasion, Mary Kay attended an all-day sales seminar and wanted to shake hands with the company's sales manager after his inspiring speech. She waited in line for *three hours*. When she finally got to shake his hand, he never even looked at her. Instead, he looked over her shoulder to see how much longer the line was. Mary Kay was sure that he wasn't even aware that he was shaking her hand.[4]

Yes, the sales manager was tired from three hours of shaking hands, but Mary Kay was tired from three hours of waiting. Hurt and offended by being treated as if she never existed, Mary Kay made a decision that day to always give people her undivided attention, no matter how tired she was. And she went on to say:

"Every person is special! I sincerely believe this. Each of us wants to feel good about himself or herself, but to me it is just as important to make others feel the same way. Whenever I meet someone, I try to imagine him wearing an invisible sign that says, 'Make me feel important!'"[5]

The Golden Rule Has a Reverse Side

There are many obvious ways to try to make the people you manage feel important and most of them are based on the Golden Rule: "Do to others as you would have them do to you."[6] One of the best ways to bolster employee morale is to give them plenty of strokes and reinforcement. As Kathleen Ryan, management consultant and best-selling business writer puts it: "The number one thing employees say they want from a manager is: Make me feel good about myself and my work. You can't change how much they get paid, but it's amazing how little it takes to build goodwill with your employees with pats on the back and kudos."[7]

As you hand out pats on the back, kudos, and other kinds of recognition, keep in mind, however, that while the Golden Rule often applies, there is a reverse side to that coin that I like to put this way:

LEMAN'S LAW #20:

**Do unto others as they want
to be done by.**

In other words, all birth orders don't necessarily want or need the same kind of recognition. Suppose, for example, you have on your team an only child who just likes to stay back in his office and work in peace. This is typical only-child behavior and many only children simply don't need a lot of strokes. On the other hand, on your staff there is also a baby of the family who thirsts for praise like a sponge.

Now let's thicken the plot by making you, the manager, a first born or only child yourself. Suppose you lean toward not needing much praise either. How is this going to affect your management? If you're not careful, you'll be appreciating those only-child employees who don't need a lot of encouragement and wondering what in the world is wrong with all those last borns who seem to be so touchy and sensitive.

To develop the mindset of a really good manager, you must always be looking behind the eyes of your team members. How do they see things? What do they really need? How do they want to be treated? When you can pull that off with regularity, you will be a great manager.

More than one management consultant will tell you that, while employee recognition is a principle that everyone agrees on, ". . . it remains one of the worst-executed management practices . . . up to ninety percent of employees say appreciation is meaningful, yet less than thirty percent say their companies appropriately appreciate them."[8]

What companies think is "appropriate appreciation" varies a great deal. At Ford Motor Company and AT&T, employees are honored by appearing in company television commercials.

At Hewlett Packard, sales people receive pistachio nuts for outstanding work.

At Random House Publishers, employees get ten free books a year.

At Macintosh, employees who worked on the very first Apple

computers were allowed to sign their names on the inside of the product.

At Federal Express, the names of employees' children are displayed on their airplanes.[9]

Some of the above ideas may sound like things you want to try; others may sound inane and ineffective. And that's the point. You need to know *your* people and what turns them on. Ideally, you should try to give recognition as individually as possible, recognizing each of your people in the way he or she prefers. When that isn't always practical, a good universal encourager is usually money, particularly if it comes in an unexpected or unique way.

Try Throwing a $50-a-Plate Dinner

While doing some consultation for a large savings and loan firm that had several branches in a midwestern city, I was talking with a vice-president who was wondering how he could get his employees to come to a *free* dinner given by the company! It seems he was charged with scheduling and programming a monthly meeting of the employees, which was designed to improve morale and esprit de corps. Sometimes it would be a full dinner, on other occasions it would be hors d'oeuvres and beverages. The catch, however, was that the meeting was always held after hours on employee time, not company time.

"I'm just not getting a good turnout," he complained. "Do you have any ideas on how I can get our people to come to these meetings?"

"I know one way that you can really get their attention," I replied. "Without saying anything, just put a $50 bill under everyone's plate at your next dinner."

The vice-president looked at me rather strangely, obviously wondering if I was saying that he *always* had to put a $50 bill under the dinner plates to get people to come out for a free meal. I explained to him, however, that he need only do this once to gain employee attention. For the next few meetings, he might not do anything, and then he might come up with some other prize (not necessarily fifty dollars) for those who would attend.

What I was giving him was a simplistic version of some basic behavioral psychology, which deals with fixed and variable interval reinforcement schedules. When training is done on a *fixed interval*, the same reward is always given. But when training is done on a *variable interval*, the reward is not always the same.

The vice-president decided to take my advice. Because only about half of the firm's one hundred or so employees came to the dinner, it cost him a little over $2,500. That was small change when compared to the annual Christmas bonus bill, and he definitely got employee attention. I heard later that attendance at the meetings radically improved after that.

There are many ways to help your people feel good about themselves and their work. There are also some ways to easily destroy all the goodwill you have built by making sudden changes without enough preparation or explanation. If anything can make people feel unimportant in a business, it's having something changed without their being notified, much less consulted. And, of course, each birth order reacts a little differently to change.

Why Change Threatens the First Born

How do you tell first borns about changes that are going to affect them, their department, their company? How do you tell them that their nice, secure, under-control world has now become less secure and maybe, for the moment at least, out of control?

You tell them very carefully. One thing first borns must understand is that in business today, change is part of life. Businesses that fail to understand the need for change are likely to die. In fact, according to Tom Peters, the word *change* is passé and now it's much more in vogue to think of *revolution*, not just change.

As Peters says, "Change? Change! Yes, we've almost all, finally, embraced the notion that 'change is the only constant.' Well, sorry. Forget change! The word is feeble. Keep saying, 'revolution.' If it doesn't roll easily off your tongue, then I suggest you have a perception problem—and, more to the point, a business or career problem."[10]

First borns, however, aren't happy with words like *change* and certainly not with something as extreme as *revolution*. They like things carved in granite. They find their comfort zone, and that's where they want to operate.

When talking to first borns about changes that are being made or about to be made, bend over backward to avoid bushwhacking them. Never forget:

LEMAN'S LAW #21:

First borns don't like surprises. Introduce change slowly and gently.

Acknowledge at the feeling level that you understand that change is very difficult for them. If you are a first born yourself, you can say you empathize but the change is still going to happen.

Make sure that you take time to train your first borns and instruct them on the new procedures or whatever the change entails. Give them a timetable—another very important item for a first born—when changes are going to be implemented. At the same time, you need to give them a certain amount of freedom to operate because they love to push ahead on their own. But give them this freedom with guidance and information. And keep them informed because they tend to be very bossy characters who want to know everything that is going on.

Middle Children Can Adapt to Change

When informing middle children of change, you're not walking in the mine field that you can so easily have with first borns. Middle children have lived their whole lives adapting to having big brother or sister getting the first shot at everything while the baby beneath them was usually spoiled and the center of attention. In a sense, "adaptable" is a middle child's middle name. That's why the statistics show that marriages involving middle children last longer. They are negotiators by nature. When presented with a change or a surprise, they don't recoil in horror or flare up with anger; they simply start to think about what they can offer in return and how they can work it out.

But while middle children will probably be easiest to deal with concerning change, there are some things you can still do to help them adapt as easily as possible. For one thing, the middle child needs to know that he or she is a valued member of the team. This may mean dropping by the middle child's desk to say just that. It can also mean doing lunch and asking about family and other personal issues that are appropriate.

Remember, too, that middle children can get lost in the shuffle because they don't make a lot of noise. The squeaky wheels often get the grease while the middle children get neglected. Don't let that happen because middle children are often the backbone of the business. They are the middle management types, the hands-on workers who can always be counted on to be steady and unflappable. These are the people who will give their best effort to the team because they have a strong sense of loyalty to the company.

I like to call the middle children the "English setters of life." In seminars I often mention that as a kid I had an English setter named "Prince." In retrospect, I am sure that Prince was a middle child—born smack in the middle of the litter for sure. At eight o'clock every morning, Prince would walk me to school through the snow and ice of western New York State winters. At 2:30 he'd be right back at the same door I'd entered that morning, ready to walk me back home again. It didn't matter what the weather was like; Prince was there because Prince was loyal.

When the winds of change blow hard on your company, your middle children are likely to be there, giving you full support. They are usually the last ones to bail out in a crisis, but never forget:

LEMAN'S LAW #22:

When instituting change, never take advantage of a middle child's loyalty.

The Babies Want to Know What's in It for Them

When it comes to introducing change to the babies of the family, you will get a couple of basic reactions. One might be, "Sounds good! It's about time we had a change around here. We haven't had one for at least a month."

More likely, however, what the last born really wants to know is, "How is this change going to affect me personally? Does this mean I'm going to wind up selling more product and earning less money? Or will it be the other way around?"

In short, last borns may look at change through a jaundiced eye and be skeptical because the change may suggest that their personal stake in things is threatened. This isn't the same problem with change that I mentioned concerning first borns. The first borns don't like change because they simply don't like change.

Youngest children in the family, however, see change in a very different light. Change can be a very real threat to babies personally. It may look to them as though their "territory" is being encroached upon; or worse, their status is being downgraded.

So if I'm managing last borns and I know changes are coming, I want their input. I want to know how they feel about it and if they think they can improve the planning that has been done so far. In short, I want to involve the babies and convince them that this is not only good for them but good for the company.

It's always smart to try to bring the baby of the family more into the bosom of the company. As a manager, every time I would have any kind of exchange with a last born, I'd do everything I could to help them see the big picture as far as the company is concerned. Babies are too easily sucked into concentrating only on themselves. They need all the help you can give them to understand that as the company benefits, they will benefit as well. Always sell babies hard on this:

LEMAN'S LAW #23:

What's good for the company is good for all of us.

Also, along this same line, be aware of the last born's "dark side"—that side that says, "I wasn't given much respect when I was little. Now I'll show you."

At their worst, babies can start firing cheap shots that can pull the company down, or if another company dangles a juicy carrot in front of them, they will be the first ones to jump at it and leave their old company in the lurch.

In short, babies are much less likely to have a conscience. In my own case, I was lucky because, although I grew up playing the role of clown/troublemaker, my parents' values, particularly my mother's, saved me from winding up with little or no conscience. That's why I was able to quit selling magazines to people who didn't need them, and set my sights on better things.

But as you work with last borns as a group, keep in mind that they may be the first who want to jump ship, the first who may give you a hard time. The question that you must ask yourself as the manager/employer is, "Would I rather have this baby of the family, who may have some shortcomings, selling *for* our company or *against* our company?"

If you want that baby of the family selling for your company, you will discover a way to explain the coming changes that will keep him functioning as part of the team instead of dragging his feet or jumping ship.

How to Provoke Change without Being Provoking

At the other end of the spectrum from selling changes to your employees is getting them to do some original thinking and suggesting changes of their own. Why should you always have to be the one who comes up with suggestions for needed changes? Your staff can be a gold mine of ideas. Sometimes people need a jump start. As I talked with my good friend Michael Lorelli, president-Americas of Tambrands, Inc., he mentioned that his staff is made to think by being "Lorellied" now and then.

"Just what does it mean to be 'Lorellied'?" I asked Michael.

"Being 'Lorellied,'" Michael responded, "means being surprised out of left field with a thought-provoking question that's in a completely different time zone."

What Michael was saying reminded me of one of my favorite bits of advice for parents with children who won't mind. I often tell Mom and Dad: "Pull the rug out and let the little buzzards tumble. In other words, lovingly but firmly make the child pay the consequences for his behavior." So I asked Mike: "Would being 'Lorellied' include pulling the rug out from underneath some-one?"

"No," Mike responded, "because that implies a negative. As opposed to pulling the rug out, being 'Lorellied' means you just hit somebody with something so bizarre that they start to think, 'Where in the world did that idea come from?' But then, after they sit back and think about it, they realize maybe it's something we should all take a look at."

"So one of your goals when you 'Lorelli' your people is to make them more divergent than convergent in their thinking?"

"Yes, absolutely. 'Thinking out of the box.' 'Seeing around the corner.' Sessions like that usually produce some of our best ideas."

Sometimes It Helps to Just "Share Your Heart"

Recently I had dropped by a fairly large retail operation that sells home appliances of all kinds in a big way. The store is really more of a glorified warehouse than anything, but every time I've been there I've noticed that the store is neat, clean, and inviting.

On this particular day I wheeled into their sprawling parking lot, and as I got out of my car I noticed a well-dressed man moving up and down the front of the store picking up papers, Dixie cups, and what have you. I recognized Bill, the owner of the place, whose titles, if he bothered to have titles, would include president, CEO, and chairman of the board.

"It's good to see the boss out working with the rest of the folks!" I called out.

Bill looked up and smiled. "Yeah, that's right. I've always done that—and I always will."

Just then somebody called out his name and he had to go into the store to take a phone call. Later, however, I talked to him again and mentioned, "Bill, I'm working on a book for business people."

"What's it about?" Bill asked.

*H*ave you ever thought about taking some of your employees aside and just sharing your heart with them? . . . Tell them about your hopes and dreams. . . . See if they don't want to become a real part of all that.

I went on to describe a few basic principles and premises. He had heard me talk about birth order on other occasions and found the concept of applying birth order to business intriguing. Then we shifted gears and started talking about all the problems of business: rising costs, theft, employees who don't produce. Bill seemed particularly irked by employees who didn't want to "get with the program." He's from the old school. In fact, he told me that at age eighteen he had sold shoes. At nineteen he had managed a restaurant.

"That explains a lot of things for me," I told him. "You've always worked hard and pulled yourself up by the bootstraps more or less. Now you look around at some of your employees and you can't understand why they don't work harder, why it's so hard to get people to do what you want them to do."

"Right! That's it exactly."

"Have you ever thought about taking some of your employees aside and just sharing your heart with them?" I suggested. "Tell them about when you used to sell shoes or manage that restaurant. Tell them about your hopes and dreams for this store. See if they don't want to become a real part of all that."

"Well," Bill mused, "I'm not sure I could do that. That sounds a little too personal."

"Well, tell you what. Maybe sometime I could come down and you could get all of your employees together in the back room and

I could get up in front with you and we could do what I call a little 'lifestyle demonstration.' With just a few questions, I can have you lay out your basic beliefs in life and I promise it won't hurt a bit."

"Thanks, Doc," Bill said. "I'll have to think about that one."

As I got back in my car, Bill had resumed picking up in front of the store, still hoping to motivate his lackluster workers by "setting a good example." As I drove away, I hoped I had at least planted a seed by suggesting that he share his heart with his staff. As hard a worker as my friend is, he won't get what he wants until he learns how to get their attention more effectively.

As badly as Bill may want to *clobber* some of his people, he needs to think more about communicating with them effectively. But just how do you communicate with employees who aren't producing the way you would like to see them produce? We'll look at that in the next chapter.

The Bottom Line

1. Do I allow for differences in my people, or do I want "everyone to do everything the same"?

2. How much risk-taking do I encourage? Am I willing to "flaunt my imperfections" and admit my own failures to my people?

3. Do I believe that managing is a relational task? What do I do that proves this to be true?

4. When I deal with my people, do I see that invisible sign that says, "Make me feel important!"?

5. Do I believe in getting my people to think by asking thought-provoking questions? How many have I asked lately?

6. Have I shared my heart with any of my people? Have I told them about my dreams for the operation and where they fit in?

CHAPTER TEN

Good Managers Get the Most from Each Birth Order

I f there are ever times when you need to communicate effectively with employees, it's when they need to see that they are not producing according to their potential or even coming close to what their job description says they need to be doing. It's then that you have to move in with some discipline—not punishment, *discipline*. If I may take a page from my counseling files, discipline is really love in action. It's firm love that guides the employee toward being accountable and responsible.

Everyone wants and needs discipline because it provides security. There is a well-known study that recorded the difference in the behavior of children on a playground without a fence and one with a fence. When the children had no fence (boundaries), they were far more inclined to misbehave. When the fence was put up, their behavior improved markedly. Be aware that adults are really overgrown children. They need fences, too.

We All Have to Make Our Own Choices

Often the difference between "handing out punishment" and "confronting with love" lies in helping someone make the right choice on his or her own. A few years ago I counseled with a hard-charging businessman whose life was a mess. He was an alcoholic whose marriage was headed for disaster. At work his alcoholism had put him on the bubble and he was about to be fired.

I had tried the usual counseling techniques, but nothing seemed to make much difference. One day I just confronted him with the need to make a choice. If he wanted to turn his marriage around and save his job, now was the time to do it. I gave him specific instructions on how to get to an excellent alcoholic treatment center in town and then I made my pitch:

"You know, I could make the call to the treatment center for you and get everything lined up, but this is really something you have to do for yourself. In fact, I don't want you to bother to make a call, I just want you to go over there and check yourself in. Now keep in mind, once you leave this office and you're on the way to the treatment center, thoughts will come into your mind to sidetrack you from ever getting to the center. You'll think of having to pick up your cleaning, the car needs an oil change, there was that errand that you're supposed to do for your wife. Put all that aside. If you really want to make a difference in your life, now is the time, but you have to do this on your own."

My client left and I have to admit I had my doubts about his resolve. I was pleasantly surprised a half hour later when he called me from the treatment center where he had just checked in. Responding to my challenge to put up or shut up, he had made a choice that literally changed his life. I didn't do anything but point out the obvious and give him some encouragement. My client is the one who made the difference for himself. But every fall around Thanksgiving time I receive a present from him in the mail—his way of saying, "Thank you."

Now what does this story have to do with disciplining people in your department or your plant? Simply this: Discipline is too often seen as something we "hand out" to offenders who need it. Surely part of discipline is dealing with someone who needs to change direction or attitude, but a bigger part is helping that person see that he or she has to walk the line alone. So often people in management positions make choices for those under their direction and then try to enforce their will upon them. Then they wonder why their employees continue to drag their feet or have a poor attitude.

I realize that your company or business may have a manual citing specific disciplinary procedures that need to be followed regarding complaints, grievances, and violations of policy. And, with all the concern about sexual harassment these days, your manual undoubtedly outlines clearly *who* should discipline *whom* and under what conditions. But before I start talking about specific ways to discipline each birth order, I'd like to lay down a few "psychological ground rules" that you might want to remember in order to be preventive in your management. That is, you want to deal with the little ripples of life before they come up; or when they do occur, you want to keep the ripples from escalating into waves.

1. As a rule, you need to give three strokes for every swat, that is, with most people it takes three or four positive remarks to offset one criticism. Some birth orders take criticism better than others. It's your job to read your people and know how much they can take and how much positive encouragement they will need if your criticisms are to do any good.

2. Never criticize an employee in public, that is, in front of other employees. In fact, go easy on "constructive remarks" in front of other employees because they are so easily interpreted as criticism. Keep in mind that even raised eyebrows can be devastating, particularly if you raise them with other people watching.

3. Do your own disciplining or dirty work, as the case may be. I still remember the president of a company who called me in to go three doors down the hall to fire his vice-president! What we

had there was definitely a failure to communicate, and then some.

4. Sometimes a big part of disciplining people is motivating them. When you have an employee who is very upset with a certain development, or a certain change that isn't boding well for him or his department, use a technique made famous by Haim Ginott, a master child psychologist who wrote several best-sellers during the '70s. Haim always liked to say: "Grant in fantasy what you cannot give in reality."

   A very good approach to use with an employee who is upset, feeling put-upon, betrayed, and so on, is: "I wish it were different. Wouldn't it be great if we could have done it that way . . ." And then go on to explain that reality is reality and help the employee move on from there.

5. Once you pursue a course of action with an employee, do not back down. Be open to his or her side and change your mind if the facts bear that out, but never let an employee's rage or sullenness intimidate you.

   One of the biggest weaknesses I see in many managers in companies where I consult is their distaste for confrontation and their willingness to back off in order to "make peace" and be a "good guy." Whenever you find it needful to discipline an employee and correct something that's wrong, gather your facts, know your ground, and then go ahead and do it, sensitively but firmly. If the employee gives you "his side," you want to maintain a fine line between standing your ground and being unreasonable. I always put it this way:

LEMAN'S LAW #24:

Stick to your guns
without shooting yourself in the foot.

In other words, hear your employee out, and if he or she makes a good point or explains what happened in a way that throws new light on a situation, you may want to change your mind. This may be a bit hard on your pride, but shooting yourself (and the company) in the foot could be a lot worse.

Discipline is confronting people with the need to change and then stepping back and letting them make the necessary changes on their own.

Disciplining, or even correcting, employees is not always easy. With some people it can be downright difficult, but it is absolutely necessary if the company is to survive in a marketplace that is more competitive than before. Yes, you want to treat every individual fairly. Yes, you want to make allowances for certain personalities, and different birth order traits and characteristics. While all of that is true, the very bottom line is this:

LEMAN'S LAW #25:

The whole is always more important than the parts.

When I asked Herb Kelleher if Southwest Airlines is more important than all the different parts of the company, he replied: "Yes, I believe that. I have always believed that it is vitally imperative that you keep your focus on that. Alfred North Whitehead has said that everything in the world is connected, even the spider that walks across its spider web has effects around the world. I've always believed that our company is an organism and that every little thing that happens affects all of us."

To sum up then, discipline is confronting people with the need to change and then stepping back and letting them make the necessary changes on their own. Obviously, some people do this better than others—some birth orders, in fact, do it better than others. Following are some tips on dealing with the various birth orders when discipline is necessary.

First Borns Are Critical but They Hate Criticism

If I as a manager have a first born who isn't living up to potential, my first guess is that it's very likely this person is getting criticism from somewhere in the organization, and the flak is making him or her stop short of giving it 100 percent. Because first borns are often perfectionistic, they are very wary of failing or even having the look of failure. One way to protect yourself from failure is not to try as hard. The reasoning goes, "If I don't put myself on the line, I probably won't get run over."

I have made my living on people who eat themselves up with self-criticism they learned at the knee of a very critical mom and/or dad.

But when a worker won't put forth his best effort out of fear of criticism, he is crippled, and so is the company. So as a manager I will come alongside and ask, "Tell me, in complete confidence, is somebody in our organization giving you a hard time in any way? Is there flak coming down to you from someone above in the chain of command? Or is it coming horizontally from someone at your level?" If your first-born employee levels with you, you may discover the source of the problem and be able to take steps to eliminate it—mainly, by confronting the person handing out the flak.

On the other hand, always keep in mind that with a first born, flak may not necessarily be coming from without. It can be raging within where it can do a lot more damage. It's not at all unusual for first borns to grow up in homes where criticism reigns because Mom and/or Dad is continually on their case.

First borns learn to set standards they can't possibly reach, but they never stop trying. They make putting themselves down into an art form and, when they reach adulthood and become fully functioning in the workplace, do they learn the folly of perfectionism? Of course not. I have made my living on people who eat themselves up with self-criticism they learned at the knee of a very critical mom and/or dad.

If you have employees who always seem to be "beating themselves up" because they can't satisfy that critical voice within, take another look at Chapter Eight, especially the ideas on page 144–45 for helping employees move from pursuing perfectionism to seeking excellence.

Always Give First Borns Specific Deadlines

One thing you need to do with first borns is give them specific deadlines. You want something on your desk by a certain date or time—no excuses. Does that sound unloving? On the contrary, it's tough love, which I like to put in these terms:

LEMAN'S LAW #26:

**Never accept excuses;
it only makes the weak weaker.**

When I taught counseling psychology classes at the University of Arizona, I had a definite policy that homework had to be in on time. Each student had to walk up and put the homework on my desk—no sending it with somebody else.

Naturally, I got every excuse in the book: They couldn't get it typed, they couldn't get into the library to do the research, a roommate borrowed it and lost it, the dog tinkled on it—you name it. But the excuses didn't help. The student got a zero for that day.

"But Doc Leman, you don't understand," my students would plead.

"I do understand," I would respond pleasantly. "Your homework isn't on my desk, and that's the rule. So you have a problem with your typist or with the library. Those are your problems, not my problems."

As soon as I communicated to my classes that I meant exactly what I said, it was amazing how homework suddenly started coming in on time. This even included homework from a six-foot-eight-inch, 285-pound defensive end on the football team. He was a good kid, but lazy as the day was long. That laziness, however, simply masked a first-born discouraged perfectionist. After I buried the bone with him and he had a few F's for a daily grade, he got the point. His assignments came in on time and he made a good grade by the end of the semester.

I realize that supervising people in a business setting isn't quite the same as making sure students get in their homework, but the parallel is still there. One good approach, particularly to a first born who isn't getting work in on time, is to say: "I'm disappointed. This just doesn't seem to be something I would expect from someone like you. Can you tell me what you think is wrong?"

Then let the first born explain. With many first borns, just stopping them and letting them know you are disappointed will be more than enough. With others, however, you have to be a bit more careful, and we'll talk about those next.

Compliant Overachievers Can Be Eaten Alive

At the other end of the spectrum, you can find the *compliant overachiever*. Compliant first borns will often let aggressive first borns walk all over them and run them ragged or into total burnout.

Why, exactly, does this happen? The answer is absurdly simple. Compliant first borns grow up wanting desperately to please Mom and Dad. Then they just branch out, wanting desperately to please teachers, coaches, Scout group leaders, employers—anyone with whom they have significant dealings, and particularly *those in authority*.

It's not that the compliant first born is necessarily afraid of those in authority; it's just that almost from Day One they have looked up to powerful figures in authority and have wanted to please them in every way possible. So, when a compliant first born falls into the clutches of an aggressive first born, the result can be sad indeed. You've probably heard this all too familiar scenario (or maybe you've lived, or are living, your own version):

First-born Marjorie has been an executive secretary to Mr. Forsythe for fourteen years. He's overbearing, selfish, demanding—a first born himself, an only child, to be exact. He continues to pile work on Marjorie and she continues to accept it. He doesn't know what he would do without her, but at the same time he treats her like dirt.

And here it is Friday night. After fourteen years you would think Marjorie had earned the right to leave a bit early on Fridays if she so desired. Tonight she definitely does so desire. Her older daughter has a lead in a play at school, and Marjorie needs to get home, get through dinner, and get down to the auditorium. But, no, here it is well after five and we find her busy at the computer finishing another huge pile of letters that Mr. Forsythe dictated at the last minute, with strict orders that, "All of these have to go out tonight, go ahead and sign my name, I've got to run."

The Abuser and the Abusee Both Need Discipline

This kind of situation needs discipline all right. But in this case both parties need to be confronted: Marjorie for her willingness to be abused and misused and Mr. Forsythe for being an overbearing jerk. Unfortunately, this kind of situation goes on all the time in businesses of all sizes across the land. In fact, it may well be that you've read this little anecdote and thought, *What's the matter with that? Isn't that what good secretaries are supposed to do?*

No, it isn't. If you're in a management position where you see this kind of thing happening—perhaps a manager one step below you is treating his secretary this way—you should move in on it, gently but firmly, to make corrections.

For example, suppose you have a "Mr. Forsythe" who is continuing to take advantage of, or even abuse, a secretary or some other worker under him or her. Call Mr. Forsythe in and explain that "Marjorie" would never come directly to you and complain, but on occasion you have found her working late after everyone has left. Tell Mr. Forsythe it appears that he is either piling on too much work or his timing is such that it always makes Marjorie work overtime on a regular basis. Let Mr. Forsythe know that he is clearly in charge of his department, and the work must go out, but you are wondering:

"I could be wrong, but I think it would be helpful to get behind your secretary's eyes to see how she views life. Ask yourself how you would want your boss to treat you. I'm not a psychologist, but just reading her body language tells me she is a depressed pleaser. She would kill herself to please you, but I'm wondering if you're not taking advantage of her. Do you really think this is the best way to get her best production?"

At this point give "Mr. Forsythe" opportunity to explain how he sees life himself. Perhaps he has had no idea that he is working Marjorie too hard. This is how it's always been and, for all you know, he thinks Marjorie feels great about everything. Once the problem is on the table, you can go on to say:

"Tell me, how has her work been recently? Would you say her accuracy and speed are up or down?"

If Forsythe tells you it's up, continue to make him aware that by working Marjorie so hard, the stress could someday cause her to snap or burn out. If Forsythe admits her accuracy and speed are down, say you are really not surprised and add: "Maybe you need a different approach. Do you have any ideas on how you could operate differently or perhaps redistribute her workload?"

Another thought to give Forsythe is that he could give Marjorie "comp time"—allow her to come in a couple of hours later on the Monday following one of those Fridays when he loaded on the work at the last minute.

As I work with my own office manager, Debbie, I constantly try to be aware of her workload, as well as her responsibilities at home. She's the mother of an only child, and when she began working for me, we both faced a problem. When Debbie's daughter was sick and had to be out of school, Debbie would bring her along to the office because she had difficulty finding proper child care.

I quickly made it clear to Debbie that whenever her daughter was sick, the best thing to do was simply close down her desk, go home, and take care of her child. She could always "make up the time" later on those hectic days when it was necessary to work past normal quitting time.

Coming back to Mr. Forsythe and trying to get him to treat Marjorie better, he may or may not come up with any brilliant plans. It may take several conversations to get him to lighten up on Marjorie, but you will have laid the groundwork and he now knows that you are aware that he is taking advantage of a compliant pleaser who is under his authority. He may get the message quickly, or it may take time. If he doesn't seem to get the message, one possibility is to give him a taste of his own medicine. As he's leaving on a Friday night, assign him a nasty job that only he can do over the weekend (so he can't rope Marjorie into helping him) and then tell him you will need his verbal report by ten o'clock Monday morning.

As for disciplining Marjorie, you need to handle this in a different way, but be every bit as confrontative about the problem. Review the advice I gave Malcolm in Chapter Two and let Marjorie know that she needs to speak up on occasion when the workload is too heavy or when everything is dumped on her at 4:35 P.M. on Friday. Assure her that you are aware of her situation and that she need not fear reprisals from her overbearing overseer. Let her know that you're pleased because she wants to please, but pleasing only goes so far and then it turns into a form of pseudomasochism that isn't healthy.

Oh, yes, perish the thought, but if you see *yourself* doing a more than average imitation of Mr. Forsythe with your own compliant secretary or other worker, you may want to consider changing your ways. Be aware that today's business climate is no longer favorable to the "good ol' boy" system. If you push an employee too hard, you can find yourself the target of a sexual harassment charge or a lawsuit of one kind or another. 'Nuff said!

Appeal to the Middle Child's Loyalty

A good approach when having to confront a middle child about lack of performance is those same telling words already mentioned: "I'm disappointed." But the goal with the middle child is to appeal to his loyalty to you and the company. Let him know you just don't understand why he is not doing his usual efficient, steady job.

True, you may put the middle child on a bit of a guilt trip, but that's okay as long as you don't overdo it. The loyalty middle children have for their company makes them feel conscientious, and to be approached by a manager who's saying he or she is disappointed can be very effective.

Another good tack with the middle child is to ask if there is something you can do to help. Is there something you are not aware of? Remember that middle children like to be secretive and keep things to themselves. There could be something or someone inside the company who is really inhibiting the middle child's production or just putting a wet blanket on life in general.

And, of course, there could be something outside the company—in the middle child's family, for example—that could be causing problems. Remember that middle children will seldom come to you and share their problems, and you will have to pry the details out of them.

One more pointer about disciplining the middle child: Never do it in front of others. This is true of any birth order, of course, but with the middle child make the confrontation as private as possible. If you want the middle child to "step into your office," try to wait until everyone else is gone. The more considerate and private you are about your correction of the middle child, the more appreciative he or she will be and the better results you will get.

Give Babies a Long Leash, but Keep a Firm Grip

Not surprisingly, last borns of the family—those "incorrigible babies"—typically need more discipline, at least more supervision, than the other birth orders. Being a baby myself, I know whereof I speak (so does my mother).

If you're managing last borns, check in with them on a regular basis. Regular could mean once a day or it could mean twice a week. If you're serious about supervising a last born, once a week might not be quite enough. Some questions you might want to ask when you check with the last born include:

- "What are you going to do today?"
- "What are you planning to get accomplished this week— what are your goals?"
- "Tell me, what are your top priorities for this month?"

This last question might throw many last borns. They usually don't think a month in advance, but it's something to expose them to now and then. One of the reasons last borns can get in trouble on budgets, deadlines, and production schedules, is that they don't look far enough ahead.

Another good question for any baby is, "Do you really believe you can meet your own expectations?" In other words, the last born has set some goals, fuzzy though they might be, and the question is, Does he really expect to reach those goals or is this all just a little game of going through the motions?

So far, I'm sure I've sounded rather severe in describing how to approach the last born. Let me temper this by saying, your goal is to be firm but still friendly and understanding. You must walk a fine line between being helpful and sounding patronizing, between being encouraging and sounding critical.

Always be aware that the last born has that dark side that may start him thinking, *I'll show you!* Your goal is to get him to show you that he can do it. But if you get the last born deep-down angry, he'll show you, all right. He'll show you what a poor job he can do, as he torpedoes your ambitions for his success.

And that's the point—you want the last born to have ambitions for his own success. Treat him firm but fair and keep as much fun in it as you can, and he will appreciate being kept on track.

I truly believe the only children and first borns of the world have been put here to keep us last borns on the straight and narrow—and most of the time I appreciate it. For example, when I talk to producers of TV shows (who are almost always first borns), I'm always careful to thank them for their direction and help. They really do know how to add structure to a six-minute interview, which is usually all you have. They understand things like a beginning, a middle, and an end. The typical last born is more inclined to think life is just one big middle, and sometimes that can turn into a muddle!

Suppose, however, that you've done your supervising very faithfully and carefully, but the last born is still blowing it. That same basic line that you use with first borns and middle children is still good here as long as you add a few flourishes. Start by saying, "I'm disappointed in you." Then add: "With your track record and your ability, I thought we wouldn't have this kind of problem. Do you have any problems that I need to know about? Is there anything I can do or get that will help you?"

Whenever you have to critique a last born, plenty of kind words are in order: "You are so capable. . . . you have natural talent. . . . I know you can do a bang-up job. . . . what's wrong? Why are your numbers [production, efficiency, etc.] falling off?"

If your last born is serious about doing a better job, he or she will respond positively and you can work from there. If, however, the last born doesn't see much need for your help, or even see exactly what the problem is, then you may have a real problem, indeed. Start probing deeper for real family problems at home, or start looking for signs of use of drugs or alcohol. Do everything you can to let the last born know that you are concerned and that you do want him or her to change. Another possible route is to ask the employee's friends or fellow workers what's going on. They may be willing to fill in some blanks.

Finally, you can always make it clear to the last born: "If I don't see a significant jump in your figures [production, efficiency] in a month, I'm going to be really concerned." Start painting the proverbial picture on the wall for the last born, and if you must, let him know: "As you know, as a company, we can't survive if this kind of thing continues. If necessary, I'll have to consider making some changes."

That last remark is, of course, strictly of the "last resort" variety. Hold it for use only after you've tried everything else.

Harvey Gives Them "The Chair"

When push comes to shove and you feel the absolute need to chew someone out, I suggest you try Harvey Mackay's approach. He gives the offender "the chair." Harvey admits that nothing works every time, but when he is really unhappy with an employee, he has his secretary summon the offender by telling him, "I've never seen Mr. Mackay so angry . . ." Then he lets him stew in the reception area for up to thirty minutes, contemplating his fate.

Finally, he is ushered in and Mackay gets up out of his chair and says, "Jack, please go over and sit in that chair."

The employee sits in Mackay's chair behind his desk while Mackay sits in what normally would be the employee's chair, and then comes the question, "All right, Jack, now what would you say if you were me?"[1]

According to Mackay, sitting in that unfamiliar spot and knowing they don't belong in that position of authority, makes the typical employee squirm. Most of those whom Harvey has given "the chair" are much harder on themselves than he ever would be. In addition, Mackay doesn't have to do any of the chewing out because the employee does all the dirty work.

Another advantage to "the chair" is that you get a chance to let the employees look behind *your eyes* to see how you feel when they mess up. After the employee has been seated in your chair and you're sitting in his, say: "I'm just wondering if you can appreciate how a manager feels when somebody fouls up. For a minute here, you're in my place and I'm in yours. Tell me what I need to hear. Give it to me straight."

When strong measures are needed, you might want to try using "the chair." Keep in mind that the typical conscientious first born will hate the chair with a passion. The middle child may be able to roll with the punches, but he, too, will feel very uncomfortable because he thinks his loyalty is being called into question. Then, of course, there's the baby. If anybody's going to be able to handle the chair, it might be the last born. In fact, some babies might just start playing with items on the top of your desk!

Harvey Mackay admits that every now and then his "chair approach" backfires. Then he has to wait until next time, and when the next time comes, he doesn't give up his chair. Instead, he fires the person who didn't get (or wouldn't receive) the message the first time.

Disciplining the three major birth orders is more or less an escalating kind of thing as far as pressure or severity is concerned. Because they are perfectionists, many first borns and only children will only need a hard look or a very gentle "swat," figuratively speaking. The typical middle child may only need a nudge or a light rap on the knuckles. The typical last born may need a little more than that, and always be sure to keep the bit in baby's mouth.

And When Somebody Dumps on You . . .

Finally, a bit of advice for you, the manager, when you get called on the carpet yourself. There is an old story whose origin has been lost long ago, but it goes like this:

There was a little bird who would spend his summers in the far north and always fly south for the winter. As he grew older, he decided that making that trip south was really getting to be a drag, and so late one summer he decided: "I'm not going to bother. I'm going to try to stick it out here over the winter."

In less than a month the little bird knew that he had made a *big* mistake. The howling winds were threatening to freeze him solid, and one day he decided that flying south made a lot of sense after all. So he took to the air, but as his little wings beat against the wind and the rain, he soon grew tired. Then the temperature dropped, and ice formed on his wings. In no time he was spiraling down, thinking to himself, *I'm a goner . . . it's all over.*

The little bird came to rest right in the middle of a farmer's barnyard. A huge milk cow ambled over, sniffed at him disinterestedly, and then walked on, almost trampling him under her huge hoofs. Just as she passed over the bird, she let go and dumped on him with a giant "cow flop"!

The little bird, who had been telling himself, "It's all over, I'm going to die, I'll never make it," suddenly felt very warm. In just a matter of seconds he started saying, "I'm going to live! I feel better! I know I'm going to make it!"

So happy was the little bird he started to chirp and to sing with sheer joy at being warmed so thoroughly by the cow plop. Life seemed good because hypothermia was no longer in his immediate future.

Suddenly, however, a big cat appeared, attracted by all the chirping and singing. He started raking away at the cow plop to see what was inside making all those birdlike noises. In a moment he had uncovered his prize, and in one gulp the little bird was lunch.

Now there are three morals to this story:

1. Everybody who dumps on you isn't necessarily your enemy.

2. Everybody who takes it off of you isn't necessarily your friend.

3. When somebody dumps on you, keep your mouth shut! You will live longer!

That's not bad advice for you or the people you manage. Let everyone in your business, company, or division know that being disciplined is not necessarily such a bad deal. Let your people know that you're not there to drive them like cattle or bully them into producing more and more while being paid less and less. Do everything you can to convince them you're there to lead, nurture, and encourage. For every manager, two old clichés, slightly paraphrased, apply:

> *Y*ou can't just drive [your people] like cattle or even herd them like sheep. You have to coax, convince, motivate, and inspire.

First, "You catch more flies with honey than just about anything." Second, "Carry a big stick but always speak softly."

Years ago when I took one of my first staff positions at the University of Arizona as a dorm director, Bill Foster, the associate dean of students, took me aside one day and gave me some advice about administrating my staff of several RAs (resident assistants) who were in charge of maintaining order among the hundreds of student residents in the dorm. "Kevin," he said, "always remember, there are 360 of them and only one of you!"

I've never forgotten Bill's words. He was telling me that a leader always has to win the cooperation of his people. You can't just drive them like cattle or even herd them like sheep. You have to coax, convince, motivate, and inspire. Sure, you can always use your stick, but it should be your last option, never your first.

Also keep in mind that bees make lots of honey when they have a plentiful supply of pollen and a fairly peaceful atmosphere. Stir up the beehive and you have nothing but trouble and lack of productivity.

One way to keep the bees in your hive happy is to employ another concept that is a watchword of the '90s—*empowerment*. We'll look next at using the pluses of empowerment, while avoiding the minuses.

The Bottom Line

1. Do I manage my people in a way that is consistent with how they view life? Can I list any recent examples?

2. Which people on my staff don't like surprises? How can I introduce them to change more gently?

3. Are any compliant first borns under my supervision being taken advantage of? Am I taking advantage of this kind of person? What can I do to change this situation?

4. How about my own birth order and how I respond to discipline? What strengths and weaknesses that I developed while growing up in my family have I brought to my task as manager? What do I need to develop more and what do I need to get rid of, or at least try to curb?

CHAPTER ELEVEN

To Keep Your Power, Give Some of It Away

Among the overused—and sometimes misunderstood—business buzzwords of the '90s is *empowerment*—putting more power in the hands of employees to make decisions, to spend money, and act decisively to get their jobs done faster, more efficiently, and, in the long run, more profitably.

As a manager—or employer—where do you stand on empowerment? At one extreme there are still some business leaders around who hold on to the view exemplified in a remark by Frank Borman, former chairman of Eastern Airlines: "I'm not going to have the monkeys running the zoo."[1]

At the other end of the spectrum is the freewheeling opinion of Michael Lorelli, president-Americas of Tambrands, Inc. When I asked him what he thought of a statement like "To keep your power, give some of it away," Mike replied, "I almost prefer to say, 'To keep your power, give almost all of it away.'"

"And how do you do that?" I asked with surprise.

"You've got to be genuine about it, but what you do is you give your people a lot of electoral votes."

"That's a good analogy," I replied. "The electoral votes idea suggests that you've hired the right people, you've put a good team together, and now you're saying, 'I'm going to give you guys the wherewithal to make this thing happen.'"

"I love when people who work for me come and ask my

*O*nce in a while you need to lose and let your people win.
—*Michael Lorelli,*
President-Americas of
Tambrands, Inc.

opinion on stuff," Mike replied. "I give them my feelings and let them know if I feel strongly or not, but I also let them know that it's their decision, which is a nice way of saying, 'Hey, John, on this issue, electorally speaking, you are Pennsylvania, New York, and California, and I'm Rhode Island and Delaware.'"

One other bit of Lorelli psychology that dovetails nicely with the need to give employees psychological ownership is his observation that: "Once in a while you need to lose and let your people win. When you lose and let your people win it drives home the fact that a ten-wheel drive beats a one-wheel drive any day. In other words, if ten people under you are pulling for you, that's a lot better than pulling the load all by yourself."

Now it's likely that your own opinion lies somewhere between Lorelli's and Borman's. Frankly, I hope you lean more toward Lorelli, who has had top-drawer positions with Pepsi-cola East, Pizza Hut, and Tambrands, Inc. Borman, an astronaut (and quite likely an extreme perfectionist), is no longer in the news as president of Eastern Airlines because Eastern Airlines is no more.

Could Borman and Eastern have survived by empowering employees more? That's hard to say, but it's a good bet that referring to Eastern employees as "monkeys" didn't do a whole lot for morale and, ultimately, profit margins.

The important thing to remember about empowerment is that the real issue is control. A business guru like Robert H. Waterman, Jr., author of *What America Does Right*, says something we psychologists have known for years: "People who feel in control of at least some part of their lives tend to be healthier, happier, and more effective. . . . One of the strongest needs each of us has is to feel that we have at least a little control over what happens to us."[2]

You've probably read or heard about the success some companies have had with the "self-managing team" concept—groups of three to ten people who work without any direct supervision. These self-directed teams make decisions on what's to be done on a given day, set their own goals, and then take responsibility for quality control, purchasing, the control of absenteeism, and employee behavior. The three to ten team members have to learn all of the jobs that fall within their group's work area.

From giant firms like Proctor and Gamble, where self-directed teams have upped productivity 30 to 40 percent, to Motorola where any assembly line worker can shut down the line if he spots the slightest problem,[3] to the Ritz-Carlton Hotel chain, where every employee, even a junior bellhop, can spend up to $2,000 on the spot to fix a guest's problem,[4] empowerment is an idea whose time has come.

If you believe you're empowering people right and left and having good results, skip the rest of this chapter and move on. But it's possible that all these super success stories notwithstanding, you're still not sure about empowerment. You may be struggling with how much power to give people at lower levels.

American Airlines Grants "Freedom with Guidance"

When I talked to Robert Crandall, chairman and president of American Airlines, he voiced the dilemma that many executives feel when it come to empowerment. When I asked him if he felt businesses were having people on the front lines make more decisions without passing the buck on up the ladder, Crandall said:

"We always have in this business. The problem is, that as we have struggled over the years to find the right balance, our people on the front lines have said to us on the one hand, 'We want the ability to decide something when we think we should.' We have said, 'Okay, you've got it.' But on the other hand, they have said to us, 'Look, we hear you telling us that we need to accommodate the customer, but we need some guidelines from you as to what is a reasonable accommodation.'"

"So, what I'm hearing," I observed, "is that empowerment isn't something you do automatically—there is a tension."

*E*mpowerment is **not so much freedom within limits, but freedom with guidance.**
—Robert Crandall,
Chairman and President,
American Airlines

"What we learned is that we simply can't take away all of the guidelines. At one point we took away every guideline and said, 'Do whatever you think is right,' and our costs went right off the chart. As we talked to people about what was wrong, they told us, 'We don't have any guidelines. We don't have any idea of what's reason-able. So tell us what's reasonable.'"

"So people want freedom but they want limits as well?"

"Not so much freedom within limits, but *freedom with guid-ance*. So what we do today is essentially say, 'Look, here are the guidelines. When you need to make a decision, you are free to deviate from the guidelines if you think it's necessary. If you are convinced you should do something else, go ahead and do it and we won't grouch at you. But under normal circumstances, these guidelines are reasonable.'"

Bob Crandall's phrase "freedom with guidance" sounded very familiar. It reminds me of a bit of wisdom I have seen work in families where parents struggle to get children to behave. Many managers are struggling to get their employees to cooperate, to function more happily and more efficiently. If that's your prob-lem, take a page from the parenting manuals. In a very real sense, parents have to *give away some of their power if they hope to keep it*. Whether you're parenting or producing a product for sale, it makes sense:

LEMAN'S LAW #27:

Place responsibility where it belongs, then ask people to be accountable.

In this simple statement lies the key to empowerment. It doesn't matter if your company is big or small, the problem of making empowerment happen can be reduced to some very basic psychology:

1. Employees want more freedom to act and think on their own.

2. Employers who grant that freedom want employees to use it responsibly.

Obviously, more trust has to be developed between employer and employee. The employer must give the employee freedom (i.e., give up power and control) and the employee must respond by showing the employer he or she can be responsible and is willing to be held accountable for what happens.

Southwest Wants Employees to Learn from Mistakes

Another airline president who grapples with empowering people and then asking them to be accountable is Herb Kelleher of Southwest Airlines. When I asked him if holding people accountable was a concept that worked at Southwest, here is how he summed it up:

"I think it's a good principle as long as it's done with understanding. We hold people accountable for what they do, we talk to them frequently about their performance or their lack thereof, but we always give them the opportunity to learn during that process. In other words, it's not, 'You did something wrong, therefore, we're going to penalize you, or discipline you, or terminate you'; instead it's 'Something went awry here and let's see if we can learn a lesson from it.'"

Kelleher went on to explain that he likes to keep in mind the famous story about Thomas Watson, CEO of IBM. When a vice-president of IBM came up with an idea to set up a separate division, he was given permission to do so and promptly lost ten million dollars. He came in and told Mr. Watson that he was resigning and when Watson asked why, the vice-president said, "Because this thing was such a miserable failure."

> *We hold people accountable. . . . we talk to them frequently about their performance . . . but we always give them the opportunity to learn during that process.*
> —Herb Kelleher, President and CEO, Southwest Airlines

Watson is reported to have responded, "You're not resigning after I just spent ten million dollars on your education."

"That's sort of the way we look at it," Kelleher commented. "Now, of course, if we see a pattern of repetitive behavior that is irresponsible or detrimental, then we know we have another problem and we try to deal with that."

The President Who Learned to Make Pizzas

If you're going to hand responsibility to people on the firing line, then you need to model responsibility yourself. One of the best ways to do this is to "get your hands dirty" doing exactly what the workers on the lower end of the totem pole do day in and day out to make the company actually run.

When he left Pepsi Cola in 1992, Mike Lorelli had four months to train before assuming his new duties at Pizza Hut. He spent those four months learning the Pizza Hut system by literally doing every job in the business. Mike told me: "I assigned myself to a Pizza Hut in Glenville, Connecticut, where I waited tables, cleaned dishes, made dough, prepared pizzas, worked at the cutting table, served pizzas, and, oh, yes, I cleaned the rest rooms."

"What kind of tips did you get?"

"Small ones. But my favorite story concerns a particular young lady who would wait on me at the Peoples' Savings Bank in my town when I was president of Pepsicola East. Whenever I did my banking, I was dressed in my usual suit and tie and she knew I was a Pepsi executive. But when I got promoted to my new position at Pizza Hut, she knew nothing about it.

"One day I was waiting on tables at the Pizza Hut down the street from her bank and this same young woman walked in with her sister. She saw me dressed in my Pizza Hut T-shirt, complete with apron, and my name badge 'M. Lorelli, Trainee.' The look on her face was classic. 'Mr. Lorelli!' she gasped, and then she just looked down at her feet. I'm not sure whether she was embarrassed for me or herself. Perhaps she thought I had lost my job and was working part-time. At that moment I realized I could 'save face' and explain to her that I was a lot more than a trainee—that I was really the new president of Pizza Hut and I was just trying to learn something about how things were done, or I could do a great job of waiting on her and her sister. I chose to do the latter."

Southwest Execs "Get out Among 'Em" Regularly

A spin-off from Lorelli's "down-and-dirty story" is the policy used at Southwest Airlines. While talking to Herb Kelleher, I mentioned that on a Southwest flight I'd seen two gentlemen walking up and down the aisles, serving peanuts and Cokes, and

> *We try to foster the idea that everybody should be willing to do everybody else's job. . . . We actually require that our officers spend one day every quarter out in the field filling someone else's position.*
> —Herb Kelleher,
> President and CEO,
> Southwest Airlines

they obviously weren't flight attendants. They looked as if they were from management somewhere, and yet they were helping out. Why?

"At Southwest we try to foster the idea that everybody should be willing to do everybody else's job," Kelleher explained. "Everybody in management is taught that there is no job they don't honor and there is no job that they should not be willing to do. We actually require that our officers spend one day every quarter out in the field filling someone else's position."

"And you do this even with your top people? Doesn't anyone think this could be a waste of time?"

"It doesn't matter who they are. They can have a superior education from a top-notch school, but we insist that they get a taste of working on the ramp, for example, handling bags, so they get a firsthand feel for what hard physical labor is like. That way they have a much better understanding of the employees who work on the ramp, how they think, and how they react to things. Working on the front lines is the first course of training at Southwest, and we insist that people keep it up regularly."

Could the principle of working on the front lines to get an employee's perspective of things work for you and other management personnel? If you're serious about making empowerment more than a buzzword, you will think about ways you can "get out among 'em and get down and dirty." The more you do so, the more you'll be able to "get behind your employees' eyes" to see how they view you, the company, and any rules you have laid down as company or department policy.

How Many Rules Are Too Many?

Josh McDowell, best-selling author and popular speaker on college campuses, is one of a handful of people I know who probably racks up more frequent flier miles than I do. I always like to quote one of his most powerful observations about life in any social organization, be it a family or a business:

Rules without relationships lead to rebellion.[5]

It goes without saying that if you don't have a relationship with the people in your company or business, telling them "here are the rules, follow them," won't work very well. Robert Crandall of American Airlines put it this way:

"I think people react very badly to rules for which they can see no reason or rules that they don't understand. I think this is one of the reasons people are often angry at government. A rule gets made, but the reasons for it are lost over the passage of time. There doesn't seem to be anybody around who can explain it, and everybody simply chants, 'Well, we have to follow the rule because the rule is there.' People get very angry about that. On the other hand, if a good relationship has been established, the reason for a rule will tend to be known, whether it's in a family or a business, and there's been some explanation or there is some understanding why that rule exists."

"What I hear you saying," I commented, "is that people simply need to know why certain rules exist—they need information. Do you think American Airlines does a good job of teaching people that?"

"In a huge corporation like ours, one of the things we've learned over time is that people want to get their guidance from a local leader. For example, a fleet service clerk or mechanic would like to get information on leadership from a first-line supervisor. Part of our problem and probably part of the problem with most big companies is that it is very hard to get enough of the right information needed for coherent leadership into the hands of the first-line supervisor. The first-line supervisor is often asked questions to which he or she simply doesn't know the answer. And if there is not some easy place to get the answer, the supervisor either has to guess or react by simply exerting authority—'Do it because I said to do it.' When our first-line supervisors slip into this authoritarian mode, it makes the job of explaining the reason for the rules more complicated. We continue to try, but my guess is that we're imperfect."

Crandall's honesty is refreshing, but it's my guess that in most companies the emphasis isn't on how perfect management is at building relationships, but whether or not management is even trying to do so. When managers are perceived as people who care, good things can happen. In other words, if rules without relationships lead to rebellion, rules with good relationships can lead to cooperation, even sweetness and light. Southwest Airlines is a good example.

They Took Stock Instead of a Raise

The night before I interviewed Herb Kelleher, he had signed a contract with all of his Southwest Airlines pilots—a ten-year agreement to accept stock options in lieu of pay increases for the entire period. In other words, Herb got all of his pilots to bet on the future of Southwest instead of asking for their regular annual or biannual raises.

During the official signing ceremony, which followed a sumptuous dinner, the pilots gave eloquent testimony to Kelleher and Southwest management as an entire team. The spokesman for the pilots said the reason they were willing to enter into the stock agreement was because they had complete trust in Southwest Airlines' management. They understood that Kelleher and other executives were looking out for the pilots' well-being, as well as the well-being of Southwest Airlines.

There is little question that Southwest's empowerment policies have a lot to do with winning the trust of their pilots, as well as the trust of the rest of their employees. Empowerment *does* work, but there are some attitudes that must be present in management if it is to work well.

Where Empowerment Always Starts

If most of the business gurus and many companies from giant corporations down to mom-and-pop operations are for empowerment, why isn't it happening on an even wider scale? Tom Peters cites two problems, both rooted in basic psychology.

First, there is the "Duke of Wellington complex"—managers who just can't give up control because they are afraid their workers will abuse being empowered and won't produce unless they, the managers, "do their job properly."

> *L*etting go means letting the person alone to experience those Maalox moments. That is, true, genuine, no-bologna ownership in the gut. If there's no deep-seated, psychological ownership, there's no ownership. Period.
> —*Tom Peters,*
> The Tom Peters Seminar

The second block to empowerment is what Peters calls "half trust," which leads to "half delegating." Managers need to be like the private pilot who observed that an instructor can't "half sit" next to you during your first solo.

"Put another way," writes Peters, "people either 'own' a task or they don't." Peters believes most bosses love to "half delegate," but what they must do instead is train their people and then *let go*—the sooner, the better.

"Letting go means letting the person alone to experience those Maalox moments," says Peters. "That is, true, genuine, no-bologna ownership in the gut. If there's no deep-seated, psychological ownership, there's no ownership. Period."[6]

Jerry Kindall Had to Learn to "Let Go"

As I do counseling in organizations of all kinds, one of the key problems I see is people in positions of authority who have had to learn how to give up control and empower the people below them. One of the best examples is Jerry Kindall, head coach of the University of Arizona baseball team since 1972.

Kindall, you may recall, is a former major league ball player who spent time with the Chicago Cubs, the Cleveland Indians, and the Minnesota Twins before going into coaching, first at the University of Minnesota and then coming to the U of A in the early '70s.

Kindall's Wildcat baseball teams have won three national championships, and when I talked to Jerry about empowerment and his own management/coaching style, he had some interesting confessions to make. When he first arrived at the University of Arizona twenty-four years ago, it was his first head-coaching job and he felt personally responsible for every Wildcat loss. Today he admits that was a big mistake. Following is part of our dialogue:

> Jerry: Frankly, I have always felt that the leadership
> rested with me, that if decisions are to be made, I
> should make them. Over the years I've evolved to
> see that there is a better way. I guess I'm a control-
> ler—I've been called that and I have to admit to
> that. I like to know who's responsible.

Kevin: You're a benevolent controller then?

Jerry: I've often thought that the most effective way of governing or leading is the benevolent monarchy. I've always felt that I know best through my experience and that the decisions I make on behalf of the team and the players are good ones. I've always tried to do right, but I've learned over the years that the more responsibility and trust that I give my assistant coaches, the better our program will be.

Kevin: Was it hard to let go at first?

Jerry: Of course. But fortunately I learned that all of us can share the responsibility. I listen much more carefully now than I used to—to the players and to the assistant coaches. And I've become a better leader because of it.

Kevin: Give me an example of how you listen more to your assistant coaches these days.

Jerry: When I was able to relinquish complete authority to my associate, Jim Wing, and let him take over developing and directing the pitchers on our Arizona baseball team, our pitching improved a great deal. Jim became a better coach because he felt more trusted and I became a better head coach because I was able to step back and put confidence in Jim's great ability.

While Kindall has learned to delegate and trust others with being responsible and accountable, he has always remained careful to never be guilty of "passing the buck."

"I've always felt that the final responsibility still rests at my door," he said. "I've never tried to avoid that."

Helping people learn from mistakes but still having "the buck stops here" sign on your desk are two keys for any executive or manager who wants to empower the people on his or her staff. The key to making people responsible and holding them accountable is not the iron hand of discipline but the helping hand of a shepherd.

How the Godparent Concept Works at Pepsi

One of the best examples I've found of shepherding the employees in an organization is the "godparent concept" that was used at Pepsicola East when Michael Lorelli was president. Lorelli describes a godparent as "someone who looks after someone else in the organization, in other words, a mentor to someone else in the company who might be working down the hall, a thousand miles away, or even in another country. The point is, you are looking after that person and that person feels that he can call on you on a confidential basis and say, 'Here's something I've been thinking about. What's your reaction?'"

When Lorelli left Pepsi, not everyone in the organization had his or her own godparent, but it's his opinion that everyone in a company should have such a person.

"The godparent concept must start at the top," Lorelli explained. "We just told ourselves that if mentorship is a good idea, it should be something that transcends an organization regardless of geography. At Pepsi, a lot of our people worked one thousand or even fifteen hundred miles away in branch offices, so we said, 'Let's create godparents and play an efficient role in their lives.'"

"It seems to me that the godparent idea suggests being a family in business," I commented. "There is a sense of coming together, of commonality in trying to get things done. It follows, then, that this is a good way to empower people, doesn't it?"

"Oh, yes, big time! Being a godparent makes you think a lot about your godchild. You think about this person regularly and have an emotional attachment. You want that person to succeed. You are quite open to letting that person cry on your shoulder. This person can call you anytime regardless of pain or hurt and not feel that confidentiality would be broken in any way, shape, or form."

"Who were the godparents when you were with Pepsi East?"

"Godparents were people who reported to me—the senior officials, such as the vice-president of sales, the vice-president of human resources, the vice-president of manufacturing, the vice-president of operations. In each case, each one of these officials broke the formal communication lines and just kept an eye out for someone lower in the organization, regardless of where that person might be located."

"If I were a godparent in your company and I was vice-president of marketing, who would be my godchild?"

"If you were vice-president of marketing, your godchild could be a sales manager in charge of distribution for Pennsylvania. The sales manager would feel very special because someone two or three levels above could put a hand out to care and call and cultivate. It's one thing to be empowered, but it's another to know that people above you are receptive. They'll take your phone calls and listen to your problems and ideas."

When I asked Lorelli if godparents ever held their godchildren accountable, he responded, "No, not really. It's more of an advisory capacity—like coaching."

"Then being a godparent and a godchild is a two-way street?"

"Absolutely. Your godchild is always free to come to you with any questions, but at the same time if you observe your godchild doing something that might be done differently or a little better, you are free to go to him or her and say something."

"Give me an example of how you godparented someone when you were at Pepsi East."

"Back when I was executive vice-president for Pepsicola North America, I was godparent to a young guy who handled new products. When I went into a field job for Pepsicola East, I remained his godparent although we worked out of different offices. Then I heard he was having an issue with his new boss because his philosophy had always been 'It's better to make a decision without your boss's permission and apologize afterward, than go in and ask for his agreement in advance.'"

"So what did you do—how did you approach him?"

"I took him aside one day and explained why his philosophy of 'get permission later' just wouldn't work anymore. Because he was at a certain level of responsibility, he was dealing with things that could have far higher impact on the company if he were wrong. His lightbulb went on."

The godparent concept may or may not be applicable in your business, but it's worth thinking about because it parallels a simple truth that a friend of mine saw emblazoned on the wall of a businessman who is a partner in a small ready-to-wear manufacturing firm. The businessman, who chose to remain anonymous, has a montage of photographs of people in his organization, and smack in the middle of all those faces is a good-sized sign that is positively profound. Frankly, this idea is so good, I got his permission to steal it and make it part of my "law library":

LEMAN'S LAW #28:

"It's the people, stupid!"

Unless you value people, godparenting, empowerment, or any other good idea won't work very well. In the next chapter, we'll take a closer look at values. What or whom do you value and why? Your own answers may surprise you.

The Bottom Line

1. Is empowering my employees (or those I manage) something I should be doing? In what ways am I empowering them already and how can I use empowerment more effectively?

2. How comfortable am I with placing responsibility where it belongs and then asking that person to be accountable? Do I really do this well or do I have difficulty? How can I improve?

3. When I hold people accountable for mistakes or errors in judgment, do I make sure they learn from the experience?

4. Would "getting out among 'em" work for me and my managerial role? What do I need to do to try to make this happen?

5. If I went to the people I manage or administrate and asked them, "Are there too many rules around here?" what would they say?

6. In my company (division, department, etc.) I make sure there are times when my people win and I lose because I value and respect their opinions.

7. Is the godparent concept a form of empowerment that we might be able to use in our organization? In what way?

CHAPTER TWELVE

Be a Winner . . .
Let the Rats Chase the Cheese

Suppose I were to come into your company to conduct a one-day seminar, and before getting under way I would sit down with someone from management and ask that person about the company's values. What kind of dialogue would take place? I've had some conversations that sounded something like this:

Manager:	Values? Well, I'm not sure. You mean stuff like honesty, integrity, fairness—things like that?
Dr. Leman:	Yes, all those are good, but what's really important? When push comes to shove, what really counts in your company?
Manager:	Oh, you mean what *really* matters? The truth be told, it would be hard work, making a profit, and winning in the marketplace.
Dr. Leman:	Okay, now that we both know where you are coming from, we can work on where you *should* be going.
Manager:	What do you mean, 'Where we *should* be going'?

At this point, I shift gears and assure the manager that I'm not insisting that the company forget hard work, winning, or making profits. It's okay to value hard work and it's okay to value winning, that's what business is all about. And it's certainly okay to value profits. Without them, you are here today, chapter eleven tomorrow.

But ahead of all those things, you need to put people. Unless you value your people as persons and not just pieces of your puzzle or cogs in your wheel, you will always be chasing the wrong rainbows. In short, the key to winning the rat race without becoming a rat is this:

LEMAN'S LAW #29:

Treat people like persons, not things.

What Is Really Involved in "Valuing People"?

As a psychologist and consultant, I spend a lot of my time trying to get people to value one another, whether the setting is a business or a family. To do this, I emphasize an area that some of my clients see as superfluous—at least at first. I'm speaking of the spiritual side of life. When a husband and a wife allow a spiritual void to occur in their own relationship, it dangerously weakens their family in many ways. Life has a way of confronting us with the tough questions about truth, right and wrong, and "morality." If there is no spiritual base, how do a mom and dad come up with any answers that make sense for the children, much less themselves?

When clients come to see me, they want to tell me about their mental and emotional problems, and possibly physical problems as well. But it's easy to see that they want the peace of mind that goes beyond the mental, emotional, or physical. When I suggest that their real problem could have a spiritual cause, their speech may become slower, even halting, their eyes will drop, and they say, "Are you talking about religion?"

I always respond that I don't want to talk about religion or jam any particular religious point of view down their throats. At the same time, I do think it's worth talking about the basic need deep within everyone on this earth—a relationship to their Creator.

I **have met people of just about every kind of faith, and I have met some who say they have no faith at all.** *I have yet to meet anyone without spiritual needs.*

I've spent over twenty-five years in counseling, speaking, and teaching in every kind of setting. I have met people of just about every kind of faith, and I have met some who say they have no faith at all. *I have yet to meet anyone without spiritual needs.*

That's why I believe that when it comes to the subject of "values," a business is no different from a family. If you want to treat people like persons and not things, you have to go back one giant step to the One who created the people. As I mentioned in Chapter One, a lot of companies are doing just that. Business leaders of different faiths are letting their beliefs have an impact on how they do business. The Bible has been taken off the shelf, dusted off, and become a guide for winning the rat race without becoming a rat.

So, if you want to set up the ideal values priority list, I suggest:

LEMAN'S LAW #30:

God first, spouse second, children third, and business fourth.

Okay, some hard-charging businessmen and -women may think that sounds naive, but hear me out. I've talked to enough business people to know that deep down they have to admit I'm right.

I talk to many people in the business world and often they are consumed with putting business first. Whenever possible, I try to pull them aside and ask them how things are going at home. I point out that you can be tremendously successful. You can sell your soul to the company store, but what if the store goes belly-up? And what happens when they no longer need you at the store? I have never heard of a CEO on his deathbed calling for his P&L sheet—he's calling for his family.

I Try to Practice What I Preach

Lest I fall into the business-before-family trap myself, I follow a stringent rule that puts my wife and children first, even if it costs money. As a platform speaker, I receive hundreds of invitations every year to go just about anywhere. I routinely turn down any requests, however, that threaten to have me on the road too long or that conflict with a birthday or other important event in our family.

Without exaggeration, I could be out almost every night of the week talking to someone, somewhere, but I don't. Why? Because my life centers on Sande and our kids, not business. I sometimes think of how ironic it would be to speak to a group of business people about being better spouses and parents if I weren't taking care of my own home front.

I recall sitting in a restaurant with my daughter Krissy when a man came over and said, "Wow, I can't imagine running into you like this. I was supposed to call you today and ask you to be the keynote speaker at our insurance convention in Phoenix on May 16—we'll be at the Camelback Inn. Can you come?"

Before I could answer, I got a sharp kick in the shin under the table and looked into the eyes of my ten-year-old daughter, whose birthday just happens to be May 16. I flinched a bit but still didn't say anything. Krissy knew she couldn't speak up at a time like this, but she let her toes do the talking with another really good kick in the very same spot.

The guy must have thought something odd was going on because I kept wincing and reaching down to rub my leg. Finally I said, "You'll have to excuse me, but the date you picked is my daughter Krissy's birthday. I can tell you right now that I wouldn't be able to come to your convention."

This kind of scene has happened more than once. In one case a CEO met with his board after I turned him down and called me back to say they had authorized him to allow my daughter to come with me, all expenses paid, if I so wished.

"You just don't get it," I replied politely. "Thank you, but no. I don't take assignments when they interfere with family celebrations."

I'm sure the CEO hung up scratching his head. I had just turned down $10,000 to stay home with my daughter and celebrate her birthday her way, and not in some hotel after Daddy got through speaking to a bunch of business people.

Before I adjust my halo and move on, I'll touch on something you may be wondering about. What about those times when you *can't* turn down the request? What about those times when the boss calls you in and says, "We need you on the East Coast by noon tomorrow? Your daughter's birthday? You'll just have to miss it this time."

I also know how this feels. Of all our children, Hannah, our fourth, is a sore spot because I missed her arrival in this world. On June 30, 1987, when Hannah was born, I was in upstate New York doing a Marriage Encounter weekend that I committed to some three years before.

Sande was a few days short of her due date when I hopped the plane for New York, hoping I'd be back in plenty of time for Hannah's birth. I spoke on Friday night, and when I got back to my room there was a message to call Tucson. I recognized the number of the medical center where my mother had worked for many years and where I had worked myself while getting through school at the U of A. As I dialed the phone, I had a growing feeling I had missed something very important.

"Oh, Leemy, she's so little," Sande's voice said from the other end of the line. To say I felt like a rat doesn't quite describe it. Sande was a doll, however, assuring me she was fine, little Hannah was fine, and I'd see them both in a couple of days.

But today, eight years later, I still have regrets. So I empathize with business people who simply have to go out of town, no ifs, ands, or buts. If that's sometimes, or even often, your plight, the key is to still stay in touch with your family—as well as refusing to go unless it's absolutely necessary.

If you do have to miss your child's birthday, some obvious suggestions include:

1. Celebrate the birthday in a big way before you go, or right after you get back, if that works out better.

2. Call her or him on that special day.

3. If it's your daughter, depending on her age, send her flowers from Daddy. My recommendation—sweatheart roses, the kind with the tiny buds. If it's your son, bring home a thoughtful gift: toy, book, fishing supplies, sports related item, cassette tape—something corresponding to his interests.

4. Plan ahead and send him or her a card with a personal note—children love to receive mail.

5. When you get back, go out of your way to make it clear to your child how badly you felt because you had to miss the birthday party or other special occasion.

My friend Michael Lorelli knows as much as anyone about having to be away from the family while traveling. I love to tell the following story, because it illustrates so perfectly what valuing your family is all about.

Traveling Again, Dad?

When Lorelli was with Pizza Hut International, he had to travel constantly—there was no other way to do the job. But as much as Michael values a job well done, he also values his family, so much so that he wrote a book for children to help them understand when their parent has to be away.

Recently, *Traveling Again, Dad?*[1] was featured in the business section of *USA Today*.[2] The "narrator" of the book is Awesome, the Lorelli family's pet hamster, now deceased. As the story unfolds, the Lorelli children track their traveling dad across the globe. Each of his destinations is marked on a map taped to the refrigerator. This leads to interesting discussions about cities, cultures, currency, government, and other lessons.

The book came out of Lorelli's own experience with having to travel so much, particularly when he was with Pizza Hut International. He wrote the text and Drew Struzan, the creator of Steven Spielberg's E.T. character, did the illustrations.

Traveling Again, Dad? was self-published by Lorelli under the banner of Awesome Books. Any profits are earmarked for some of his favorite children's charities—further proof of how he values people. Lorelli really didn't have time for the book project, but he did it anyway.

But What About Valuing Fellow Workers?

Having your values straight at home will play a major role in how you value those with whom you work. I'm not talking about appreciating their value to the company, per se. That's important, of course, but the bottom-line question is, "How valuable are your employees and coworkers as *persons*, made in God's image just as you are?"

If you want to value people completely, you have to value their opinions, their feelings, their hopes, their dreams, even their nightmares. Along with all *that*, you value their worth and service.

When Mike Lorelli was a top dog at Pizza Hut, one of his favorite people was Mary, the cleaning woman. He would stop and talk to her and spend as much time with her as anybody else he would bump into in the hallways of Pizza Hut's corporate offices. Later, as life often turns out, he learned that Mary's brother is the same person who does his lawn and yard work. One day Mary's brother stopped him and said, "Mr. Lorelli, you're one of my favorite people in the world because you give time to my sister, Mary, who cleans in your building."

When Lorelli told me this story, I commented, "I think this is getting right down to why you are the way you are and what has really made you successful in business. An attitude that is willing to spend time with Mary is an attitude that will reach out and enfold everyone."

Herb Kelleher—"Arthur Fiedler of the Skies"

Mike Lorelli's attitude toward his people reminds me of Herb Kelleher, president of Southwest Airlines. I call Herb the "Arthur Fiedler of the Skies," because he makes such beautiful music in his personal relating style—particularly with his employees.

"I've always enjoyed people—without any real effort, as a matter of fact," Kelleher told me. "In high school and college I was elected president of my class and the student body, even though I didn't seek those positions. I've always just enjoyed spending time with people. A problem they have around Southwest is that when I've visiting one of our facilities, they can't get me to leave because I'm so busy talking with people—at the counters, out on the line, anywhere. They literally have to drag me off. In fact, everyone has permission to grab me by the arm and rip off my coat sleeve, if need be, to get me to move on."

The more I talked to Kelleher the more I understood that it is no coincidence that the stock exchange symbol for Southwest Airlines is "LUV." According to Kelleher, from the very beginning Southwest has been known as the "LUV airline."

When I asked Kelleher what he had learned about life while growing up in his family, he particularly emphasized "being optimistic and idealistic at the same time."

*W*e tell prospective employees, "We're not interested in your education, experience, or expertise as much as we are your basic philosophy, your attitude toward life, whether you enjoy helping other people and serving them. If you have that attitude, we can give you almost anything else you need."
—*Herb Kelleher,*
President and CEO,
Southwest Airlines

"Who'd you get that from?"

"I think primarily from my mother, but to a certain extent from my father. He died when I was twelve. They both taught me to always watch out for those who are weaker or smaller than you are. They were both very compassionate people."

"It's obvious that you've brought a lot of your parents' philosophy of life right into your business," I observed. "If I'm not mistaken, one of your slogans is 'We hire great attitudes.' Where exactly did that phrase come from?"

"I really drew that from a statement that I heard Tom Landry make when the Dallas Cowboys were in their ascendancy. Landry said that the Cowboys draft good athletes—they can teach them to play any position they want them to play, but first they want great athletes."

"Interesting, but what does that have to do with attitude?"

"All I did was adapt Landry's statement and convert it to say, 'We hire great attitudes.' We tell people that we can teach them to perform any position within the company, wherever we need them. But if they have a lousy attitude, we're not capable of changing that. We tell prospective employees, 'We're not interested in your education, experience, or expertise as much as we are your basic philosophy, your attitude toward life, if you enjoy helping other people and serving them. If you have that attitude, we can give you almost anything else you need.'"

How to Respond When a Customer Is Wrong

I have watched Southwest employees under fire and can testify that Kelleher's words ring true. Just a few days before interviewing him, I was catching a Southwest flight for Tucson, and as I got up to the reservation counter I noticed that the ticket agents were being berated by a very irate customer. The guy looked like a cross between the village idiot and a terrorist, so I leaned in to hear what was going on. If I had gotten any closer, my nose could have been in serious danger of being rearranged on my face.

The irate gentleman had a problem with a refund he wanted put on a credit card. The trouble was, the ticket had been purchased with his mother's credit card and he wanted the refund credited to *his* account. He also wanted to get on another Southwest flight that was leaving soon.

The three Southwest ticket agents dealing with the man were trying to explain that this just wasn't possible, but as they tried to reason with him, his voice rose higher and higher until finally he was just plain screaming and yelling loud enough to be heard a hundred yards away. Finally, just as a security officer came over to see what was going on, one of the Southwest ticket agents simply handed the man cash as a refund for his ticket and said politely, "Sir, why don't you just go fly with another airline?"

When I told Herb Kelleher this story, he responded, "I don't know if you are aware of this or not, Kevin, but at Southwest we don't necessarily believe 'the customer is *always* right.' I always say it's really an injustice to your own people to say that the customer can *never* be wrong. I know of one case where a passenger hit one of our customer service agents over the head—with a briefcase, I believe. Am I supposed to say that customer was right? You can carry this 'customer is always right' business to the point where you can denigrate your own people. So I tell our employees that sometimes the customer is wrong—particularly if he tries to abuse, upbraid, or mistreat them. They're instructed to do what they can for irate customers, but not to stand there and just take endless abuse."

Bravo to Herb Kelleher for having the guts to say that some customers could be wrong and to empower his people with the right to deal with them firmly in the face of unreasonable abuse while remaining polite and professional! I can still remember how I and several other passengers witnessed this whole scene, our mouths agape. We watched the man storm off, wondering how these three Southwest employees could take all that garbage without firing a single shot in return. It was a study on how to keep your professional cool.

Two Rules Everyone Can Live With

In Herb Kelleher's opinion, being a value-oriented company is imperative. There must be no discrimination against anyone at any time. Managers are instructed to always address the issue, not the person. At Southwest Airlines, they live by two rules: (1) Treat everybody fairly; (2) Never humiliate anybody. True, there is nothing profound in these two rules. They've been around for thousands of years. But it's *living* them and *applying* them that have a profound effect.

Kelleher works hard on communicating his values to his people, and recently he enjoyed a serendipity that told him his efforts have been paying off. An expert on rating how effective communication is within corporations had Herb fill out a questionnaire, giving his opinion on a vast number of things connected with Southwest Airlines. Then, without telling anyone in the company what he was doing, the expert went around and asked a number of other Southwest people—from top management down to middle management through the lower echelons—to fill out the same questionnaire.

After getting back all the responses, the communication expert compared them to Kelleher's questionnaire. He came back to the Southwest CEO and said, "Herb, it's unbelievable. I've been doing this for twenty-two years and I've never seen a congruence on corporate values anywhere near this one. All your people told me exactly what you had said."

What's really nice about this story is that Herb Kelleher doesn't run Southwest Airlines like a gestapo general. He doesn't go around saying things or sending memos that sound like: "You *vil* have these values or ve have vays of *dealing* vit you!" He knows that "corporate congruence" comes from constant efforts to communicate positively on an upbeat basis (i.e., when you love people, they love you back).

Says Kelleher: "We make an effort to communicate: 'These are our values, these are our goals, this is where we're trying to go, this is how we're going to get there.' That way, everybody has a clear understanding of what we're all about and what we're trying to become."

Always Recognize Employee Worth and Service

Because I travel so much, I make it a point to send congratulatory letters to airlines and other companies that give me good service. When I called Southwest Airlines to see if it would be possible to get a telephone interview with the president, it was my good fortune to be directed to Vickie Shuler, Herb Kelleher's personal assistant. She was so gracious and so helpful that I just had to drop a note of congratulations to Herb to let him know what a jewel he had working for him.

Not to be outdone, Herb sent Vickie his own memorandum to let her know how much he appreciated her worth and service to the company. Note that he also included the name of Colleen Barrett, Southwest's executive vice-president of customers. A reproduction of the actual memo appears below:

March 8, 1995

MEMORANDUM

TO: Vickie Shuler
FROM: Herb and Colleen
RE: Commendation

    Whewww...Doctor Kevin Leman left our chairs spinning from such an
outstanding commendation...and we LUVed reading it! We would like to thank
you for going that "extra mile"; but, Vickie, you've added a few feet to
it, and we don't know what to call it...other than..."POSITIVELY OUTRAGEOUS
SERVICE"!!

    THANKS A MILLION FOR LETTING YOUR SOUTHWEST SPIRIT SHINE!

HDK/CCB/ksn   *Herb & Colleen*

Copy to:
     Kevin Leman

Not every company exec responds to commendatory letters from customers with the speed and enthusiasm of Herb Kelleher. On another occasion, I sent a letter of commendation to a large insurance company after being "rescued" by one of their agents in rather dramatic fashion. The story bears repeating because it illustrates how the corporate mills can sometimes grind at a glacier's pace.

How a "Good Neighbor" Rescued the Cub

It was a Friday morning and my lovely wife, Sande, was about to leave on errands that would take until late afternoon. Most of our five children were off somewhere—at college, high school, or grade school. Sande was a little nervous about leaving our fifth child, baby Lauren, then three months old, with The Cub, but I assured her that everything would be fine.

To prove to Sande that I was indeed in control, I put baby Lauren in one of those little windup swings that gently began rocking her back and forth. Unconvinced, Sande began giving me a whole litany of instructions: "Here are the Pampers. There are two bottles in the fridge, also some bananas and squash. I've got it all ready for you."

Feeling just a bit patronized, I replied reassuringly, "Honey, it's *okay*. I'm Lauren's daddy, I can take care of her. Just go ahead and enjoy your day. Don't worry about a thing."

Sande's taillights had barely faded from the end of our rather long driveway to the street below when I remembered I had to go outside and turn on a hose to water some plants. Barefoot and clad only in my Skivvies, I left little Lauren swinging away in our bedroom, chortling happily, and went out to turn on the water. When I tried to come back into the house, I found the back door had locked itself behind me.

No problem, I thought. *Surely the front door is open because Sande just left by that door and I'm sure she wouldn't have the foresight to have locked it.*

I went around to the front door and discovered that Sande had indeed locked it.

I stood at our front door in my underwear, an intrepid last born refusing to panic. *Not to worry,* I told myself. *Certainly there will be an open window somewhere.* But a quick survey of the windows proved that they were all sealed tighter than Fort Knox.

Then I remembered: *The garage door opener! There must be one in my car!*

A quick look in my car proved that, no, the garage door opener wasn't there. And then I recalled why. I had taken it inside to replace a used-up battery and had left it on a bench.

So there I was prowling outside my house barefoot in my Skivvies, unable to find an open door or window. My optimism faded as I realized there was *no way* into the house. I scrambled up on a retaining wall and peeked a look into the bedroom where I had left Lauren. There she was, still swinging, but now fast asleep. I thanked the good Lord that she wasn't screaming her head off, but I knew that time was running out. She could wake up at any second.

What could I do? I scanned our neighborhood, and, of course, like most American neighborhoods on a weekday morning, people were all working and no one was home. As I gazed across the wash at one of our neighbor's backyards, a good three-wood shot away, I noticed some workmen who were busy doing some landscaping.

Braving rocks, stickers, thorns, and other sharp objects unfriendly to bare feet, I tiptoed through the wash (actually, we call them arroyos here in Tucson). As I made my way gingerly among the scrubby little mesquite trees, I also kept a sharp eye out for various unfriendly reptiles that inhabit our Arizona desert.

Scrambling up my neighbor's bank, I limped up to the workmen and quickly discovered neither of them could speak English.

As they looked at me rather strangely, I searched my memory, trying to plug into my days as a University of Arizona student who had studied some Spanish.

"*Telefono, por favor, telefono, por favor,*" I said with a big smile in a pleading voice.

They got my message and pointed into the garage. There, miraculously, on the wall was a phone! As the workers jabbered in Spanish, I hurried across the driveway in my J. C. Penney's striped undies as fast as my chubby legs and scratched feet would carry me. I got to the phone and asked myself, *Who are you going to call? 911? After all, this is an emergency and your three-month-old baby is locked in your house.*

I decided against 911 and opted for none other than my State Farm agent. Why a State Farm agent? Obviously, because he's always your Good Neighbor! I dialed the number of Joe Robinette, who was not only my State Farm agent but a good friend as well. Joe wasn't home but his wife, Teri, answered and relayed a description of my plight to Joe on his car phone. Joe wasted no time. He called a locksmith from his car and gave him all the necessary information while en route to my house. By the time I had limped back across the arroyo and was scrambling up my own bank, Joe was turning into my driveway.

Joe hung around, roaring with laughter at times, but still sympathetic. The locksmith finally got there and sixty-five dollars later I was in my house. I dashed into the bedroom where I had left Lauren swinging and found her—still fast asleep.

So grateful was I to Joe that I forgave him for laughing at my plight (after swearing him to absolute secrecy—Sande could never know, at least for a while). The very next day I sent the whole story to the CEO of State Farm with many commendatory comments about how their agent, my Good Neighbor, had saved my bacon.

Two or three weeks went by and I finally received a reply from State Farm, thanking me for my letter and telling me they were glad one of their agents was able to help.

I looked at the reply in disbelief and told myself if I were the CEO of State Farm I would have done something very different about a letter and a story like the one I had just sent.

Two more months went by and then another letter arrived from State Farm, this time asking me for permission to use my letter and story in their company newsletter. They wanted to make their agents aware of what had happened because they could see that what Joe Robinette had done for me was the kind of service that all State Farm agents should be willing to give at any time, anywhere.

I called Joe and let him know what his company was going to do. He was pleased and so was I, of course, but with all due respect to State Farm, one of the truly fine insurance institutions in our country, I still think they missed the boat. They could have put the whole thing on television and turned it into one of the best commercials they had ever done.

From a business standpoint, the moral of this story is not: "Never get locked out of your house in your undies with your baby inside." The real point is that when one of your employees does something special, outstanding, or maybe even fairly ordinary, *make something out of it*. Get the story out any way you can: in a company newsletter, a memo to your entire staff, in a notice on the bulletin board, or at least by word of mouth. The important thing is to let your employees know they are important and valuable, and when they make news you want everyone to know about it.

But there is one little sequel to my story. I decided never to tell Sande about being locked out after she had given me all those careful instructions. Unless or until she reads about it in this book, she'll never know what happened!

Can You Value Winning Without Becoming a Rat?

We can talk about values until we're out of blue chips. We can sincerely say we want to value people and treat them like persons, not things. We want to value their opinions and their feelings, as well as their worth and their service. But deep down at the inevitable bottom line we have to value winning. Business is about making profits, and by the very definition profits mean winning—at least to some degree.

It's refreshing when a CEO of a large corporation comes right out and admits that winning is what business is all about. When I asked Robert Crandall to give me a basic principle or two with which he leads American Airlines, he said, "I'll try, but it's hard to distill the complexities and ambiguities of life down to those kinds of statements. I do think, however, that any successful business leader has got to have an overwhelming need and desire for commercial victory. You've got to, simply have to, want to win very badly. I think that the concept of winning lies at the very heart of a lot of other stuff."

"Anything else?"

"Second, I think it is tremendously important that any leader have absolute integrity, that you simply refuse to compromise the fundamental integrity of your position and your

Any successful business leader has got to have an overwhelming need and desire for commercial victory. You've got to, simply have to, want to win very badly. . . . Second, it is tremendously important that any leader have absolute integrity, that you simply refuse to compromise.
—Robert Crandall, Chairman and President, American Airlines

commercial activities. In businesses like ours, where safety is so important, everyone has to know that the company, their leaders, and they, themselves, are all expected to behave with integrity."

Crandall's answer helps explain the motto of American Airlines, which is displayed above the concourse in the Dallas/Ft. Worth airport:

Cooperation, communication, mutual respect, trust.
Working together towards excellence!

When I mentioned the sign, he said, "We do try to hold and practice those values. When we commit to do something, we do it. If we make a contract, we keep it. If we make a promise, we keep it. I think it is important, in fact, it is crucial, to always do these fundamental things."

I believe Robert Crandall's approach nicely answers the question, "Can you value winning without becoming a rat?" Yes, as long as you maintain integrity, never cutting corners to "win at any price."

For Pat Williams, *Winning* Is the Magic Word

Of all the leaders I talked to while researching this book, no one has to be more concerned about winning than Pat Williams, general manager of the Orlando Magic. First-born male in his family (he has an older sister and two younger sisters), Pat made sports his life while growing up—particularly baseball. After playing ball at Wake Forest, he signed with the Philadelphia Phillies and spent two years with a Class B farm team.

Pat soon saw that the jump to professional baseball was more than he could handle. Realizing that he was "in the twilight of a very mediocre career," Pat took a front office job in the Phillies farm team system.[3]

After five years of operating minor league baseball teams, two significant things happened for Pat Williams: (1) He became a committed Christian; (2) He was offered an opportunity to leave baseball and go into the NBA as business manager with the Philadelphia '76ers. From that day on, he has been with several NBA teams in a managerial role of some kind.

When I asked Pat what part values play in the life of the head of an NBA franchise, he said, "My whole adult life has been consumed with winning. I'm not diminishing values, playing fairly, and sticking with the rules. And I'm certainly not advocating any kind of cheating to get advantage, but I still have to say this: In professional sports, all they pay off on is winning. Every morning for thirty-three years I've had to put my feet on the floor and be concerned about winning. That's all they care about ultimately. Winning games and selling tickets."

"What I hear you saying, then," I interjected, "is that there's nothing wrong with wanting to win and wanting it very badly. If you don't want to win, why be in the league?"

"During the years I helped operate minor league baseball teams and then all of those NBA teams, including the Orlando Magic for the last ten years, winning has been a consuming passion. No, I don't apologize for winning."

How to Tell Your Kids about Winning

Winning at the NBA level is one thing, but I wondered what Pat Williams, father of eighteen children (four natural, fourteen adopted), thought about the emphasis on winning that is often shoved down the throats of kids, in Little League, for example.

How does he deal with his own children when it comes to the sticky subject of competition? What kind of kids is he raising to some day enter the world of business where they will have to swim with the sharks and try to keep from being eaten alive?

"Kevin, that's interesting," Pat replied. "I was at an Amway convention the other night, and one of the motivational speakers told a story about how he was playing some board game with his eleven-year-old son. He beat his son eleven straight times and then suggested it was time for bed. The eleven-year-old said, 'Daddy, I'm not going to bed. We're going to play another one.' The dad kept insisting it was time for bed and finally the boy said, 'Dad, you don't understand. It ain't over 'til I win.'"

"So what happened?" I asked, truly curious about when the kid got to bed.

"As the story went, when they played the twelfth game, the kid won," Pat explained. "Then I could see what this speaker was doing. Getting about ten thousand Amway people rocking and rolling: 'It ain't over! Turn to the person on your left! It ain't over 'til I win! Turn to that fellow behind you and tell him the same thing—It ain't over 'til I win!'"

"Do you think that's a good philosophy to teach kids?"

"I used that story as an illustration at the breakfast table this morning. I talked to the kids about winning, and I told them, 'You're going to school every day. You're competing in sports and going to practice. You're doing all those jobs we've assigned you to do around the house. I'll tell you why you're doing all that. It's all designed so that when you're an adult you'll be able to win, that you can be victorious in what you do, whether you're a doctor, or a lawyer, or a dentist, or an accountant. I don't know what it is

I don't know what it is you're going to be doing, but whoever hires you to do a job for them will want you to produce a victory. In other words, in any business, the operation has to be a winning operation. You've got to want to win the thing. Life pays off in victories.
—*Advice to his children by Pat Williams, General Manager, Orlando Magic*

you're going to be doing, but whoever hires you to do a job for them will want you to produce a victory. In other words, in any business, the operation has to be a winning operation. You've got to want to win the thing. Life pays off in victories.'"

I like Pat Williams's approach. I recommend it for any parent—or for any manager. It's the manager's job to communicate the need to win—not at any price, not by cutting corners, lying, shading the truth—but by giving whatever you do everything you've got all the time.

The Cheese Just Isn't Worth It

When it comes to sorting values, some of the best advice I've ever heard came from Michael Lorelli. We were chatting about how to be successful and I joked, "It's easy—just work half days."

Mike knew what I meant because he had heard me say it before in a meeting I had with his sales managers. "Right," he chuckled, "any twelve hours that you choose."

We were being facetious, of course, but at the same time a lot of business people do work "half days," and sometimes longer.

Lorelli put the balance between hard work and family well when he told me, "We need to recognize the softer side of life. I believe very strongly myself in taking three weeks of family vacation every year. I think it's symbolic. My advice is, 'Be yourself and let the rats chase the cheese. You'll be better at your work the remaining forty-nine weeks.'"

"What does that say to you as a businessman, Mike?" I asked, looking for some great psychological significance in his comment. "What do you

> *L*ife is too short. Just be yourself, have some fun, and let the crazies who are trying to prove something to the world chase the cheese. . . . If you're not having fun, it isn't worth it.
> —*Michael Lorelli,*
> *President-Americas,*
> *Tambrands, Inc.*

mean when you say, 'Be yourself and let the rats chase the cheese'?"

"Life is too short," Lorelli said quickly. "Just be yourself, have some fun, and let the crazies who are trying to prove something to the world chase the cheese. You only go around once. If you're not having fun, it isn't worth it."

The Bottom Line

1. What are my real values (what I actually do and how I actually live)?

2. What are my company's real values?

3. How do I match up with a priority system that says God first, wife second, children third, business fourth?

4. In what ways do I show people in my organization that I value them?

5. When was the last time I wrote a commendatory letter or note to one of the people I manage or employ?

6. How important is winning for me? How far do I go to win?

Portrait of a Winner

This book is based on a simple premise: Prudent people can and do win the rat race without becoming rats. In fact, they often go the second mile and avoid the rat race altogether because they know the trouble with the rat race is that, when the race is over, you're still a rat.

For me, no one is a better example of a true winner than Jerry Kindall. I've known Jerry ever since he came to Tucson for spring training while playing with the Cleveland Indians in 1962. When he was named head coach of the University of Arizona baseball team ten years later, we struck up a firm friendship.

My admiration for Jerry's coaching skills grew quickly, but I soon became even more intrigued by his fortitude, determination, and leadership. A sincere believer in God, Jerry practiced his Christian faith—not only at church but on the diamond and elsewhere.

I must admit I admired one other thing about Jerry—the huge championship ring he won while playing with the Minnesota Twins. In 1965 Jerry was the second baseman on the Twins team that won an American League pennant. All athletes of any major sport covet getting a ring that signifies they are champions. Jerry's ring was a gorgeous piece of work, solid gold with a large diamond embedded in the center. It was so big it could be seen across any room, and he wore it frequently, understandably proud of the accomplishment it stood for.

The years rolled by and Jerry began compiling a fabulous

record as coach of the Wildcats baseball team. One day in 1980 I ran into his wife, Georgia, at church and noticed she was wearing a lovely diamond pendant on a gold chain.

"Georgia, that's a beautiful pendant!" I commented.

"Well, didn't I tell you about this?" she responded. "My Jerry gave it to me!"

The more I looked at the pendant, the more familiar something seemed to be. Our eyes met and intuitively I said, "Not The Ring?"

I asked the question almost fearfully. Because of what the ring stood for—utter excellence in a certain field—I'm not at all sure that I could have given up even part of it had it been mine. Did he have to sacrifice The Ring?

Georgia told me that Jerry had indeed used the diamond from his championship ring and that the rest had been cut up and made into gold pins for his four children!

I walked away shaking my head, but then I began remembering that I had known Jerry for almost eighteen years. I knew what kind of a man he was—an inspirational leader and teacher of young men on the baseball diamond, a devoted father and husband, and a faithful, truly humble church member who loved God with all his heart. Hard as it was for me to believe a man could take his American League championship ring and cut it up, I had to admit that if there was a man on this earth who could give up a material memento, no matter how priceless, it was Jerry Kindall.

I treasured this story for many years, hoping I could use it someday at the perfect time. As I began working on this book, I realized that time had come. I went to talk with Jerry to get more details on how and why he had decided to cut up his ring and give it away as gifts to his family.

"I decided to do it while sitting in church one Sunday morning," he told me. "As I sat there fingering my ring, I suddenly realized how unworthy I was of all the blessings God had given me, particularly my family. Then the thought struck me, *Because this ring means so much to me, I should share it with those I love.*"

For the next few days, Jerry hoped that Georgia wouldn't notice that he wasn't wearing his ring. He took it to a local jeweler who removed the diamond from the center to be made into the pendant with the gold chain. Then the rest of the ring was cut up and melted down.

With the gold, the jeweler made two pendants of circle designs for Jerry's daughters and two rectangular pendants for his sons. Each child's name appeared on a pendant: Betsy, 17, was a senior in high school at the time; Doug, 15, was a sophomore; Bruce, 13, was an eighth grader; and Martha, 11, was in sixth grade.

Because the ring had become gifts for the whole family, Jerry picked a family time to present them. He chose to do it after dinner, after family devotions, with everyone there.

First, he gave the diamond pendant to Georgia, who sat there for a few seconds simply stunned with the enormity of what the gift stood for. Then tears of joy flowed because she knew how much that championship ring had meant to her husband. The older children knew as well, and they were deeply moved.

"The younger kids?" recalls Jerry. "They were just happy to have something made of gold with their names on it."

"How did you feel when you gave away your ring to the family?" I asked Jerry.

"It felt wonderful," he replied. "I couldn't stop thinking about how good God had been to me. It was something I had to do."

In 1984, Georgia contracted ALS—Lou Gehrig's disease. Her health failed rapidly, but she still accompanied Jerry and the Arizona team to the College World Series in 1986. Because I'm a devoted Wildcat fan and baseball is really my favorite sport, I went along.

I still remember being in the dugout at Rosenblatt Stadium in Omaha, Nebraska, after Arizona had suffered its first loss in the tournament. Although gravely ill, Georgia had made the trip and she was there in the dugout also. She had worn a light windbreaker, but the Omaha winds were brisk and biting. Rain was in the air and she was starting to shiver.

As reporters gathered around Jerry to get his insights into why the Wildcats had been beaten, he took off his baseball jacket and put it over his wife's shoulders. After sitting down and putting his arm around her, he turned to answer the reporters' questions.

I remember watching him—the protective loving husband, plying his trade as coach of a major college baseball team, taking defeat in stride, answering questions politely and insightfully as he had to talk about why his team had lost. I knew that Jerry Kindall didn't like to lose, but I also knew that, win or lose, he would be gracious.

The interview over, we all rode back to the hotel in silence. Arizona had lost one game, but they were still in the hunt. The Wildcats would come back and win the round-robin College World Series of 1986 by walloping Florida State in the final game, 10-3.

Georgia died the following summer, June 27, 1987, on the same weekend our fourth child, Hannah, was born. The funeral service was sad, yes, but it was also inspiring. The overflow crowd was a testimony to the lives of Georgia and Jerry Kindall. In Jerry's words, it was "a triumphant heaven-bound celebration of Georgia's life."

Life has gone on for Jerry Kindall and God has continued to bless him—with a record number of wins as Arizona's coach, and his lovely second wife, Diane. As Jerry said, "I've been blessed with *two* precious, godly wives." He's also seen all four of his children have outstanding careers in school and go on to become compassionate adults with families of their own.

In my business I have rubbed shoulders with many outstanding people. Some are rich, famous, and talented. Others are humble, caring, brilliant examples of leadership. But I can clearly say, of all the people I've ever met, there's not one I respect more than Jerry Kindall.

I've seen Jerry in the joyous times and the devastating sad times, and always he exudes dignity, goodwill, honesty, and integrity—in one word, *class*. And the symbol of all the things that Jerry Kindall is can be seen in The Ring. I don't mean The Ring he wore proudly on his finger for all those years. I'm talking about The Ring that became special gifts of tremendous meaning to those he loved the most. Those gifts symbolize the real man who is Jerry Kindall.

We could easily say Jerry knows all about winning the rat race but, truth be told, he has never even bothered to enter. He had better things to do.

NOTES

Chapter 1

1. Harvey Mackay, *Swim With the Sharks Without Being Eaten Alive* (New York: Ivy Books, 1988), 23.
2. Harvey Mackay, *Beware the Naked Man Who Offers You His Shirt* (New York: Ivy Books, 1990), 24.
3. *World News Tonight with Peter Jennings*, ABC-TV, New York, 4-8 September 1995.
4. Ibid.

Chapter 2

1. Mackay, *Beware the Naked Man Who Offers You His Shirt*, 259.
2. Alfred Adler, *Understanding Human Nature* (New York: Fawcett World Library, 1969), 127.
3. Mark Stevens, *King Icahn* (New York: Dutton, 1993), 267.
4. Karen Peterson, "Kids without Siblings Get Their Due," *USA Today*, 1 March 1993, 1D.

Chapter 3

1. Craig Horowitz, "Trump Gets Lucky," *New York*, 15 August 1994, 22.
2. Donald J. Trump with Tony Schwartz, *Trump: The Art of the Deal* (New York: Random House, 1987), 48-49. Also, Jerome Tuccille, *Trump: The Saga of America's Most Powerful Real Estate Baron* (New York: Donald I. Fine, Inc., 1985), 33.
3. Trump, *Trump: The Art of the Deal*, 3.
4. Bradford Wilson and George Edington, *First Child, Second Child* (New York: McGraw-Hill, 1981), 234-35.
5. Stephen M. Pollan and Mark Levine, *The Total Negotiator* (New York: Avon Books, 1994), 6.
6. Kevin Leman, *The Birth Order Book* (New York: Dell, 1987), 127-28.
7. Trump, *Trump: The Art of the Deal*, 43-44.

Chapter 4

1. Mackay, *Beware the Naked Man Who Offers You His Shirt*, 198.
2. Tom Peters, "'Personality' Has Southwest Flying above Its Competition," *Arizona Daily Star*, 26 September 1994, B4.

3. Thomas J. Watson, Jr., and Peter Petre, *Father, Son, and Company: My Life at IBM and Beyond* (New York: Bantam Books, 1990), 172-80.
4. Lee Iococca with William Novak, *Iococca* (New York: Bantam Books, 1986), 18.
5. Ibid., 4.

Chapter 5

1. Bill Johnson et al., "Managing and Selling Different People Differently," 7502 N. 10th Street, Phoenix, AZ 85020.
2. Mackay, *Swim With the Sharks Without Being Eaten Alive*, 28-34.
3. David Stipp, "Family Matters: Blame the Birth Order for History's Revolts, This MIT Scholar Says," *Wall Street Journal*, 23 August 1994, A1.

Chapter 6

1. Tom Peters, *Thriving on Chaos: Handbook for a Management Revolution* (New York: Random House Audio Books, 1987).
2. Derrick C. Schnebelt, "Turning the Tables," *Sales and Marketing Management*, January 1993, 22.
3. Mackay, *Swim With the Sharks*, 48-49.
4. Ibid., 53.
5. Tom Incantalupo, "Women Better at Selling Cars, Study Says," *Tucson Daily Citizen*, 9 November 1994, 9C.

Chapter 7

1. Martin John Yate, *Hiring the Best* (Boston: Bob Adams, Inc., 1987), 18-19.

Chapter 8

1. David Stoop, *Living with a Perfectionist* (Nashville: Thomas Nelson, 1987), chap. 2.
2. John Maxwell, "Eleven Keys to Excellence," as quoted in *Heartline Newsletter*, December 1993. Maxwell is the founder of INJOY, 1530 Jamacha Road, Suite D, El Cajon, CA 92019, 1-800-333-6506.

Chapter 9

1. Peters, *Thriving on Chaos*, 320.
2. From the business card of Terry Paulson, business consultant, P.O. Box 365, Agoura, CA 91376. When contacted, Paulson explained that he heard this quotation during a TV interview of hockey great Wayne Gretzky, who was relating what one of his former coaches would tell him when he failed to shoot as often as the coach thought he should.
3. Mary Kay Ash, *Mary Kay on People Management* (New York: Warner Books, 1984), 4.
4. Ibid., 4-5.
5. Ibid., 15.
6. Luke 6:31 NIV.

7. Vanessa Ho, "These Times Are Tough on Bosses, Too," *Arizona Daily Star*, 19 January 1996, C7.

8. Gerald Graham, "Employee Recognition Pays if It's Spontaneous, Sincere," *Tucson Daily Citizen*, 2 January 1995, D4.

9. Bob Nelson, *1001 Ways to Reward Employees* (New York: Workman Publishing Co., Inc., 1994).

10. Tom Peters, *The Tom Peters Seminar* (New York: Vintage Books, 1994), 8.

Chapter 10

1. Mackay, *Swim With the Sharks*, 175-76.

Chapter 11

1. Peters, *Thriving on Chaos*, 343.

2. Robert H. Waterman, Jr., *What America Does Right* (New York: W. W. Norton, 1994), 18, 32.

3. Ibid., 32, 33.

4. Peters, *The Tom Peters Seminar*, 78.

5. Josh McDowell and Dick Day, *How to Be a Hero to Your Kids* (Dallas: Word Publishing, 1991), 28.

6. Peters, *The Tom Peters Seminar,* 80-81.

Chapter 12

1. Mike Lorelli, *Traveling Again, Dad?* (Darien, Conn.: Awesome Books, 1996). To order the book, call 1-800-266-5564.

2. Rhonda Richards and Donna Rosato, "Family Turns Travel into Children's Book," *USA Today*, 7 November 1995.

3. Pat and Jill Williams with Jerry Jenkins, *Rekindled* (Grand Rapids: Fleming H. Revell, 1985), 48-49.

ABOUT THE AUTHOR

For information regarding speaking engagements
or seminars, please write or call:

Dr. Kevin Leman
7355 N. Oracle Road, Suite 205
Tucson, AZ 85704

Phone (520) 797-3830
Fax (520) 797-3809

SPECIAL SALES

Thomas Nelson books are available at special
quantity discounts for bulk purchases for sales
promotions, premiums, fund raising or educational
use. Special books or book excerpts can also be
created to fit specific needs.
For details, write or telephone Ted Squires,
Nelson Resource Management, Thomas Nelson
Publishers, P.O. Box 141000, Nashville, Tennessee
37214-1000. Phone (615) 889-9000, extension 2160

The *Doctor Is In* . . . Advice from America's Parenting Expert

Kids who have a healthy self-image are kids who weather the storms of childhood and grow up to be confident, capable, and responsible adults. *Bringing Up Kids Without Tearing Them Down* is packed with tools you need to underwrite your kids' lives with a solid sense of self-worth and confidence. At the end of each chapter, you'll find steps to follow in your own family, plus self-evaluating questions that help you gain insight into your own parenting style. Also included is a question-and-answer section to quickly reference specific problem areas.
0-7852-7806-0 • *384 pages* • *Paperback*

What happens when you marry someone who has two children—one older than your firstborn son and one younger? Who is junior now? The firstborn? The middle child? *Living in a Step-Family Without Getting Stepped On* reveals as families are blended, shuffled, and rearranged, birth orders are anything but static. When children from two families are brought together by the marriage of their parents, all of them are plunged into what Dr. Leman calls the birth order blender. Leman says, "The principles of this book will help you wage the battle of blending your family—and come up not only a survivor but a winner!"
0-8407-3492-1 • *288 pages* • *Hardcover*
Also available on audio—0-7852-8089-8

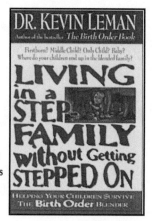

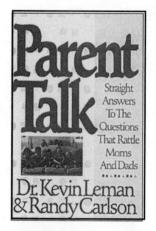

With all the vim, vigor and vitality of their live call-in radio show, nationally known radio hosts Dr. Kevin Leman and Randy Carlson have compiled some of the most-asked parenting questions from their syndicated program. *Parent Talk* shows you how to use Reality Discipline—the secret to being a good parent—to teach children with love and limits, to hold them accountable for their actions and to raise adults, not children.
0-8407-3447-6 • *320 pages* • *Hardcover*